SUNSET
WITH GOD

Quiet Moments with God

Sunset with God
ISBN: 979-8-88898-127-6 - *Paperback*
ISBN: 979-8-88898-128-3 - *Hardcover*
ISBN: 979-8-88898-129-0 - *Ebook*

Copyright © 2024 by Honor Books
Racine, WI

Cover Design by Faille Schmitz
Manuscript prepared by W. B. Freeman Concepts, Inc.,
Tulsa, Oklahoma.

When Day Is Past

By the end of the day, most of us are completely exhausted. Our bodies are tired, our energy is depleted, and our minds are empty. Creative ideas, workable solutions, and wise answers are nowhere to be found. Our emotions are frayed and our ability to communicate and relate to others is almost nonexistent.

In the midst of your weariness, take time for the Lord. Don't shut Him out, thinking that prayer or devotional time is just "one more thing" and you're just too tired. Embrace your time with Him as a life-giving respite.

"But they that wait upon the Lord shall renew their strength; they shall mount up with wings as eagles; they shall run, and not be weary; and they shall walk, and not faint."
ISAIAH 40:31

In the following pages you will find devotions that will help you to "wait" upon the Lord with faith, expecting Him to:

- give you sweet sleep,
- heal your wounds,
- calm your fears,
- restore your hope,
- renew your body, mind, and spirit,
- and give you courage to face a new tomorrow.

The Lord is your Creator. He is also your Re-Creator! He knows how you're made and He knows how to fix you when you wear out, break down, or blow a fuse.

Tonight, trust the Lord to pour himself into you, filling you to overflowing with His divine presence. He will infuse you with His strength, His power, His wisdom, His love—His life! You'll go to bed engulfed in peace and awake refreshed because you've spent *Sunset With God*!

The Power of Prayer

And when he [Jesus] had sent the multitudes away, he went up into a mountain apart to pray: and when the evening was come, he was there alone.
MATTHEW 14:23

Small children are often taught to say their evening prayers by learning a prayer such as "Now I lay me down to sleep." Although teaching children to pray is good, the "roteness" that is often learned can lead to the devaluation of this very precious and important time with the Lord.

Because evening is wind-down time, we may think our prayers lack the power and conviction that is available earlier in the day. However, prayer at any time of the day can have a powerful effect on our world. For instance:

Queen Mary said she feared the prayers of John Knox more than she feared all the armies of Scotland.

John Wesley's prayers brought revival to England, sparing them the horrors of the French Revolution.

Revival spread throughout the American colonies when Jonathan Edwards prayed.

Time after time, history has been shaped by prayer. The Rev. Billy Graham says, "I tell you, history could be altered and changed again if people went to their knees in believing prayer . . . Today we have learned to harness the power of the atom, but very few of us have learned how to develop fully the power of prayer. We have not yet learned that a man can be more powerful on his knees than behind the most powerful weapons that can be developed."[1]

Matthew 14:23 tells us Jesus sought to be alone with the Father after what must have been an extremely taxing day of preaching, teaching, and healing the multitudes. Perhaps our prayers are more powerful when weariness causes us to drop the pretenses of "religious" language in favor of direct communication with the God into Whose hands we've placed our lives.

Tonight, speak honestly and openly with the Lord about your concerns, and make your petitions known. Then cast the care of them onto Him and sleep in peace, knowing He is at work on your behalf.

───────────────

Evening and Morning

And there was evening, and there was morning – the first day.
GENESIS 1:5 NIV

In the Book of Genesis, each day of creation is concluded with the phrase, "and there was evening, and there was morning."

From the Hebrew perspective, the day begins at evening, specifically with the setting of the sun. How unlike our Western tradition, where we start our days at the crack of dawn and consider night to be the end of a long day.

What does it mean for the day to begin at evening? For Hebrew people through the centuries, the transition from afternoon to evening has been marked by prayer. "Evening prayer" is a Jewish custom. After prayer, families gather together for a meal.

The most holy day of the week, the Sabbath, begins with the lighting of candles and a proclamation of faith, then a more formal family dinner. After the evening meal, Jewish families traditionally gather together to read Gods Word and discuss how His laws apply to their lives. The evening ends in rest.

Consider the priorities evidenced by their way of life:

First, a focus upon prayer and one's relationship with God.

Second, an emphasis on family life.

Third, a daily study of Scripture, making God's Word the last thoughts of the day.

Fourth, rest and sleep.

It was only after a Hebrew talked with God, enjoyed the love and fellowship of family, studied the Scriptures, and rested, that work was undertaken!

What would happen in your life if you adopted this strategy for your evening hours? Is it possible you would find yourself more renewed and refreshed, more energetic and healthy, more creative and productive? Might the priorities you desire in your life become a reality?

Why not give it a try? Begin your next day in the evening, and wake up knowing you're totally refreshed—spirit, soul, and body—to have a full and productive day!

———————————

Night Watch

You are my hope, O Lord God.
PSALM 71:5 NKJV

Václav Havel is a former president of what used to be Czechoslovakia. In 1948 the Communists took power in his country and confiscated his family land holdings. From that time, Havel was part of a defiant underground that opposed the Soviet government.

When the Soviets marched into Prague twenty years later, Havel remained to form a coalition that would gather strength and be ready to take over when the time was right. He spoke out boldly, writing defiantly against communism. He was put under surveillance and eventually jailed for his activities.

In 1970, several US senators met with Havel in Czechoslovakia. They brought what they thought would be good news for him. They told him they intended to press for legislation allowing dissidents like himself to emigrate to the West.

Havel replied by saying he was not interested in going to the West. "What good would that do?" he asked. "Only by staying here and struggling here can we ever hope to change things." Like a watchmen in the night, Havel stayed on duty in his country.

Times of trial and struggle often seem like long, dark nights. But doing the right thing—even the hard thing—gives us hope. How do we maintain those long night watches when there seems to be little change in our circumstances?

1.   Take one step at a time. Don't attempt to tackle the whole task at once. "A man's steps are directed by the Lord" (Proverbs 20:24 NIV).

2.   Keep your struggles in perspective. Separate the mountains from the molehills. "What then shall we say to these things? If God be for us, who can be against us?" (Romans 8:31 NIV).

3.   Cultivate the discipline of delayed gratification. "But let patience have her perfect work, that ye may be perfect and entire, wanting nothing" James 1:4).

4.   Learn to recognize the invisible God in the world around you. "By faith he [Abraham] left Egypt, not fearing the king's anger; for he persevered because he saw him who is invisible" (Hebrews 11:27 NIV).[2]

Placing your hope in the Lord helps you to do all these things. He will lead you, He will remove your mountains, He will strengthen you, helping you to be patient, and He will open your eyes to His works all around you.

Leave It to Me

*Cast your burden on the Lord [releasing the weight of it] and
He will sustain you.*
PSALM 55:22 AMP

Many people find it easier to commit their future into the Lord's hands than to commit the problems and concerns of the day. We recognize our helplessness in regard to the future, but we often feel as if the present is in our own hands.

A Christian by the name of Mary Ellen once had a great burden in her life. She was so distraught she could not sleep or eat, was jeopardizing her physical and emotional health, and was on the verge of a nervous breakdown. She recognized, however, that there wasn't anything *she* could do to change her circumstances.

Then Mary Ellen read a story in a magazine about another woman, Connie, who also had major difficulties in her life. In the account, a friend asked Connie how she was able to bear up under the load of such troubles. Connie replied, "I take my problems to the Lord."

Connies friend replied, "Of course, that is what we should do."

Then Connie added, "But we must not only take our problems there. We must *leave* our problems with the Lord."[3]

Not only are we to leave our problems with the Lord, but we are to hold nothing back.

There is a humorous story about an elderly man who vowed he would never ride in an airplane. However, one day an emergency arose and it was necessary for him to get to a distant city in a hurry. The fastest way to get there was by air, of course, so he purchased a ticket and made his first trip in an airplane.

Knowing his reluctance to fly, when his relatives met him at the airport, they asked him how he enjoyed the flight. He responded, "Oh, it was all right, I guess. But I'll tell you one thing. I never let my *full weight* down on the seat."[4]

The Lord wants you to cast your burdens on Him—and leave them there! He desires for you to give Him the full weight of your problems as well. Then you can go on with life in full confidence He will take care of those things you have entrusted to Him.

Quality Time

Thou wilt show me the path of life: in thy presence is fullness of joy.
PSALM 16:11

Busy—so busy! The sun has long since set and there is still so much to do. Work, family, church, and much more seem to demand hours God never put in the day. Still, we Christians think all these accomplishments will please our heavenly Father. After all, faith without works is dead, right?

When we finally fall into bed at night, can we say we've actually spent any time with the Father we're trying so hard to please?

In his book, *Unto the Hills*, Billy Graham tells a story about a little girl and her father who were great friends and enjoyed spending time together. They went for walks and shared a passion for watching birds, enjoying the changing seasons, and meeting people who crossed their path.

One day, the father noticed a change in his daughter. If he went for a walk, she excused herself from going. Knowing she was growing up, he rationalized that she must be expected to lose interest in her Daddy as she made other friends. Nevertheless, her absence grieved him deeply.

Because of his daughter's absences, he was not in a particularly happy mood on his birthday. Then she presented him with a pair of exquisitely worked slippers, which she had hand made for him while he was out of the house walking.

At last he understood and said, "My darling, I like these slippers very much, but next time buy the slippers and let me have you all the days. I would rather have my child than anything she can make for me."[5]

Is it possible our heavenly Father sometimes feels lonely for the company of His children? Are we so busy doing good that we forget—or are too weary—to spend some quiet time with Him as our day draws to a close?

Take a walk with your heavenly Father as the sun sets. Spend some quality time, talking to Him about anything and everything. You will be blessed and so will He!

Early to Bed

O God, You are my God; early will I seek You.
PSALM 63:1 NKJV

Most of us are familiar with the old saying: "Early to bed and early to rise, Makes a man healthy and wealthy and wise." And there are numerous references in the Bible to the joys and benefits of rising early. The psalmist said,

"My heart is steadfast, O God, my heart is steadfast;
I will sing and give praise. Awake, my glory!
Awake, lute and harp! I will awaken the dawn. "
PSALM 57:7-8 NKJV

The clear implication is that the psalmist had a habit of getting up before dawn and "singing in" the morning. But what does this have to do with our sunset hours?

Very practically speaking, in order to be able to rise early in the morning, we have to get to bed early. There is no substitute for sleep. According to modern sleep research, most people need seven to ten hours of sleep a day, and lost hours can never be made up.

Sufficient sleep is the foremost factor in a person's ability to sustain a high performance level, cope with stress, and feel a sense of satisfaction in life. Getting enough sleep directly impacts our moods and emotions, our ability to think creatively and respond quickly, and our ability to sustain exertion. It is as vital to our health as what we eat and drink.

More good news about sleep and our health is that every hour of sleep we get before midnight is twice as beneficial as the hours after midnight!

A good night's sleep is one of God's blessings to you. Sufficient sleep was a part of His design for your body and His plan for your life. When you make a habit of retiring early, you put yourself in a position to receive this blessing. You'll find it easier to rise early and seek the Lord for wisdom and strength for the day ahead.

The Night Sky

*I consider Thy heavens, the work of Thy fingers, the moon
and the stars, which Thou hast ordained.*
PSALM 8:3 NASB

When was the last time you gazed up into the star-filled sky on a clear night? Do you wonder what it would be like to travel in the heavens among the stars? What lies beyond what your physical eyes can see?

Jamie Buckingham described a night like that in the snowy mountains of North Carolina:

"I walked up the dark, snow-covered road toward Cowee Bald. The sky had cleared, revealing a billion stars twinkling in the clear, cold night. The only sound was the gurgling of a small mountain stream beside the road and the soft crunch of my shoes in the snow. All the other night noises were smothered, leaving me with the impression of standing alone on earth.

"I wondered about the time, but to glance at my watch would have been sacrilegious. Clocks, calendars, automobiles, and airplanes—instruments of time and speed — were all buried beneath nature's cloak of stillness and slowness. I kicked the snow off my boot, and standing in the middle of the road, threw my head back and breathed deeply of the pine-scented air. Looking into the heavens I could see stars whose light had left there a million years ago, and realized I was just glimpsing the edge of space. Beyond that was infinity — and surrounding it all, the Creator.

"I remembered a quote from the German philosopher, Kant. Something about two irrefutable evidences of the existence of God: the moral law within and the starry universe above. I breathed His name: 'God.'

"Then, overwhelmed by His presence, I called Him what I had learned to call Him through experience: 'Father!'"[6]

Tonight, contemplate the stars in the heavens. You will find there a glimpse of eternity. What an awesome thought: *The Creator of the universe invites me to have a personal relationship with Him!*

———————————

Come Home

For this son of mine was dead and is alive again; he was lost and is found.
LUKE 15:24 NIV

Once there was a widow who lived in a miserable attic with her son. Years before, the woman had married against her parents' wishes and had gone to live in a foreign land with her husband.

Her husband had proved irresponsible and unfaithful, and after a few years he died without having made any provision for her and their child. It was with the utmost difficulty that she managed to scrape together the bare necessities of life.

The happiest times in the child's life were when the mother took him in her arms and told him about her father's house in the old country. She told him of the grassy lawn, the noble trees, the wild flowers, the lovely paintings, and the delicious meals.

The child had never seen his grandfathers home, but to him it was the most beautiful place in all the world. He longed for the time when he would go to live there.

One day the postman knocked at the attic door. The mother recognized the handwriting on the envelope, and with trembling fingers she broke the seal. There was a check and a slip of paper with just two words: "Come home."[7]

Like this father—and the father of the prodigal son—our heavenly Father opens His arms to receive us back into a place of spiritual comfort and restoration at the end of a weary day.

God does not ask us to stand and take our punishment for the days failures. He simply welcomes us into His healing presence as children redeemed by the blood of His Son. There, He assures us that He understands our hurts and shortcomings and, miracle of all miracles, loves us anyway.

The Father is calling you to come home. Why not finish your day in the comfort and provision of His presence?

Evening Praise

God is light, and in him is no darkness at all.
1 JOHN 1:5

The Book of Common Prayer has a service of Evening Prayer, which includes an ancient hymn called "Phos hilaraon" or "O Gracious Light:"

O gracious Light,
pure brightness of the everliving Father in heaven,
O Jesus Christ, holy and blessed!

Now as we come to the setting of the sun,
and our eyes behold the vesper light,
we sing your praises, O God:
Father, Son, and Holy Spirit.

You are worthy at all times to be praised by happy voices,
O Son of God, O Giver of life,
and to be glorified through all the worlds.

This ancient hymn calls our attention to the fact that although the sun may be going down, God's light never leaves us. He is with us always, day and night.

Ancient pagans believed that night was a time of death and sadness, of a "departure of the gods" from the world. This hymn proclaims the exact opposite. Jesus Christ gives life around the clock. The Father never abandons His children and He is worthy of praise at all times.

In the book of Revelation, John describes the New Jerusalem, our eternal home, with these words:

"There shall be no night there; and they need no candle, neither light of the sun; for the Lord God giveth them light: and they shall reign for ever and ever."
REVELATION 22:5

Scientists today tell us if anything is reduced to its purest form of energy, it becomes light and heat—the sun in miniature. The Gospel tells us the Son of God is our unending supply of energy and life.

He is Who and What nothing else can provide! He is the essence of all of life's energy. You can count on Him to bring light, even in your darkest night.

True Riches

Don't store up treasures on earth!
MATTHEW 6:19 CEV

They were married as soon as they graduated from college. They both were smart, attractive, and voted "most likely to succeed" by their peers. Within two decades, they had reached some pretty lofty rungs on the ladder of success: three children who attended private schools, a mansion, two luxury cars, a vacation house on the lake, a prolific investment portfolio, and the respect of all who knew them. If you had asked them what was most important in life, they would have reeled off a list of all they owned, the places they had been, and the things they had done. Success was sweet, and money made their world go round.

It will probably come as no surprise to you to learn that one day the bottom dropped out of this couple's life. They had personally guaranteed a business loan, assuming that their partners were as trustworthy as they. Not so. One partner embezzled nearly half a million dollars, and this Couple-Who-Had-It-All started down the road to becoming the Couple-Who-Lost-It-All. In the midst of their problems, the police came to their door late one night to tell them their oldest son had been killed in a car accident.

This couple discovered something vitally important in the course of putting their lives back together. A neighbor invited them to church, and thinking that they had nothing to lose by going, they started attending, eventually becoming regular members. To their amazement, they found they were enjoying Bible study, making lots of genuine friends, and feeling accepted for who they were—not for what they had in the way of material possessions. Their children also found a place to belong (no designer jeans required).[8]

Ideally, none of us will have to lose it all in order to find it all. In fact, our heavenly Father wants us to live abundantly. Keeping our priorities straight, remembering to put God first and others ahead of ourselves, is the key to sweet sleep at night!

Get Understanding

Incline your ear to wisdom, and apply your heart to understanding.
PROVERBS 2:2 NKJV

———————————————

Sometimes it seems life is lived backwards! When we are young and have only a limited perspective, we have to make the huge decisions of life that will shape the rest of our years. But we can—and are wise to—learn from those who have gained insight from life's experiences.

In a sociological study, fifty people over the age of ninety-five were asked the question: If you could live your life over again, what would you do differently? Three general responses emerged from the questionnaire.

If I had it to do over again . . .

- I would reflect more.
- I would risk more.
- I would do more things that would live on after I am dead.[9]

An elderly woman wrote this about how she would live her life if she had it to live over again:

"I'd make more mistakes next time; I'd relax; I would limber up; I would be sillier than I have been this trip; I would take fewer things seriously; I would take more chances; I would climb more mountains and swim more rivers; I would eat more ice cream and less beans; I would perhaps have more actual troubles, but I'd have fewer imaginary ones.

"You see, I'm one of those people who lives sensibly and sanely hour after hour, day after day. Oh, I've had my moments, and if I had it to do over again, I'd have more of them. In fact, I'd try to do nothing else, just moments, one after the other instead of living so many years ahead of time."[10]

Listen and learn! Life cannot be all work and no play, and yet you want your life to be meaningful, to God, to your loved ones who follow you, and to yourself.

Reflect on your life tonight. Ask God to show you the true meaning of your existence, what you are to accomplish — and how to have fun along the way!

Everyday Needs

This is the confidence we have in approaching God: that if we ask anything according to his will, he hears us. And if we know that he hears us – whatever we ask – we know that we have what we asked of him.
1 JOHN 5:14-15 NIV

"Oh, no! We're going to have to run for the ferry again!" Elaine cried. "And, unless we find a parking place in the next minute or two, we're never going to make it!"

As Elaine and her daughter, Cathy, struggled through the downtown Seattle traffic, she thought back to when they had moved to Bainbridge Island four years earlier. They had thought it to be a perfect, idyllic place, and it was while her daughter was in high school and she could work part time at home.

Now college bills had made full-time work a necessity for Elaine. She, her husband, and Cathy were obliged to make the daily commute to Seattle via the ferry. With a car parked on both sides of the water, praying for parking spaces had become a daily event.

"I told you we needed to get away from your office sooner," Cathy chided. "You just can't count on finding a parking place within walking distance of the ferry when the waterfront is full of summer tourists and conventioneers!"

"God knew about that last-minute customer I had, and He knows we have to make this ferry in order to get home in time to fix dinner and make it to the church meeting," Elaine assured her. Then she prayed aloud, "Lord, we'll circle this block one more time. Please have someone back out or we're not going to make it."

"Mom, there it is!" Cathy shouted, as they rounded the last corner. "Those people just got in their car. I have to admit—sometimes you have a lot more faith than I do. Who'd think God would be interested in whether or not we find a parking place?"

"But that's the exciting part of it," Elaine explained. "God is interested in every part of our lives—even schedules and parking places. Now, let's run for it!"[11]

The Lord knows all the circumstances of your day —and your tomorrow. Trust Him to be the "Lord of the details."

———————————————

Final Meditation

This book of the law shall not depart out of thy mouth; but thou shalt meditate therein day and night, that thou mayest observe to do according to all that is written therein: for then thou shalt make thy way prosperous, and then thou shalt have good success.
JOSHUA 1:8

One of the translations for the word "meditate" in Hebrew, the language in which the Old Testament was written, is the verb "to mutter" — to voice under ones breath, to continually repeat something. When we are taught to meditate upon the Lord and His Word day and night, we are to repeat Gods Word to ourselves continually. When we do this, Gods Word becomes foremost in our thinking. It becomes our mind-set, our world view, our perspective on life.

The Scriptures promise that when we think and speak in accordance with God's law, we will act accordingly. Thus we will enjoy success and prosperity!

In the opinion of Henry Ward Beecher, a great preacher from the 1800s, "A few moments with God at that calm and tranquil season, are of more value than much fine gold."

The psalmist proclaimed, "My mouth shall praise thee with joyful lips: when I remember thee upon my bed, and meditate on thee in the night watches" (Psalm 63:5-6).

Have your last conscious thoughts before sleeping about Gods Word. Turn off the late show, close the novel, put away the work, and rest in the Lord, recalling His Word. You'll find it easier to do this if you choose a passage of Scripture on which to meditate in the morning and then meditate upon it all day — muttering phrases and verses to yourself in the odd moments of your schedule. Then, just before you fall asleep, remind yourself one final time of Gods truth.

Those who do this report a more restful night. A peaceful mind focused on God's Word seems to produce peaceful sleep and deep relaxation for the body. In this day and age, with nearly a billion dollars spent each year on sleep aids, we have the greatest sleep aid of all — the Word of God!

———————————————

Satisfaction

In Your presence is fullness of joy.
P S A L M   1 6 : 1 1   N K J V

"Satisfaction guaranteed!" promise the ads for a new car, a refreshing soft drink, or a stay at an exotic resort. There is no end to the commercial world's promises of fulfilled hopes and dreams.

Do you know many truly satisfied people? Would you describe our culture as satisfied?

If you answer no, you're not alone. Author Max Lucado doesn't think so either. He said, "That is one thing we are not. We are not satisfied . . ."

After Thanksgiving dinner we declare, "I'm satisfied." In reality, we are probably more than satisfied! But before the end of the day's football games we are back in the kitchen digging in to the leftovers.

We plan and save for years for the "perfect vacation." We head off to our dream-come-true destination, indulge every desire for fun, food, and fantasy, and in two weeks we are headed home with wonderful memories. It may have been a satisfying two weeks, but are we fulfilled for the rest of our life when the vacation is over?

Perhaps you worked to build the home of your dreams—the place where you are king and reign over every affordable luxury and creature comfort. Does it truly satisfy your deepest desires?

Satisfaction is hard to obtain. Contentment eludes us. We are promised fulfillment many times a day, but the promises become empty after we have "taken the bite" a few times. There is nothing on earth that can satisfy our deepest longing.

In *Mere Christianity*, C. S. Lewis wrote: "If I find in myself a desire which no experience in this world can satisfy, the most probable explanation is that I was made for another world."

We were made for another world—heaven! The desire for satisfaction is very strong in our lives. However, Scripture tells us there is only one thing that will satisfy: "For in him we live, and move, and have our being; as certain also of your own poets have said, For we are also his offspring" (Acts 17:28).

—————————

His Promise of Peace

Be still, and know that I am God.
P S A L M   46:10

A woman who grew up on a large farm in Pennsylvania fondly remembers some special times with her father. Because the growing and harvest seasons were pretty much over from November through March, she recalls thinking that her father set aside that time each year just to be with her.

"During the winter months," she says, "Dad didn't have to work as hard and long as he did the rest of the year. In fact, it seemed like there were some times when he didn't work at all as far as I could tell.

"During those long winter months, he had a habit of sitting by the fire. He never refused my bid to climb up on his lap and he rewarded my effort by holding me close for hours at a time. Often, he would read to me, or invite me to read a story to him. Sometimes I would fall asleep as we talked about all the things that are important to dads and little girls. Other times, we didn't talk at all. We just gazed at the fire and enjoyed the warmth of our closeness. Oh, how I treasured those intimate moments.

"As I grew, I thought it odd that other kids dreaded the indoor days of winter. For me they meant the incredible pleasure of having my father very nearly all to myself."[12]

Just as winter is Gods season of rest for the earth, we sometimes experience "winter" in our spiritual lives. The world may seem a cold place. Like children who dread "indoor days," we can feel stifled and penned in by these spiritual winters.

If you are going through a dry, wintry time, why not snuggle close to the heavenly Father tonight, and listen to His gentle voice? The love and comfort He wants to give you will surely warm your heart!

———————————————

Cradled

Now will I arise, saith the Lord; I will set him in safety from him that puffeth at him.
P S A L M 12:5

A number of years ago, two young women boarded a ferry to cross the English Channel from England to France. About halfway through their five-hour journey, the ferry hit rough waters and a crew member later told them they were experiencing one of the roughest seas of the year! The ferry tossed about rather violently on the waves, to the point where even the seasoned crew felt ill.

At the time the ferry hit rough water, the two women were eating a light lunch in the back of the boat. They quickly put their sandwiches away. One woman lamented, "It's hard to eat while you're riding on the back of a bucking bronco!"

When it became apparent that the pitching of the boat was not going to abate, one of the women decided to return to her assigned seat in the middle of the ferry. She soon fell sound asleep and experienced no more sea sickness. Toward the end of the trip, after the ferry had moved into calmer waters off the coast of France, the other woman joined her. "That was awful," she exclaimed. "I was nauseous for two hours!"

"I'm sorry to hear that," said the second woman, almost ashamed to admit that she hadn't suffered as her friend had.

"Weren't you sick?" the first woman asked in amazement. "No," her friend admitted. "Here at our seats I must have been at the fulcrum of the boat's motion. I could see the front and back of the boat were moving up and down violently, but here, the motion was relatively calm. I simply imagined myself being rocked in the arms of God, and I fell asleep."

All around you today, life may have been unsettling and stormy, your entire life bouncing about on rough waters. But when you return to the "center" of your life, the Lord, He will set you in safety. Let Him rock you gently to sleep, and trust Him to bring you through the rough waters tomorrow.

He Keeps Us Singing

He put a new song in my mouth, a song of praise to our
God. Many will see and fear, and put their trust in the Lord.
PSALM 40:3 NRSV

Evangelist and singer N. B. Vandall sat quietly in his living room reading his paper when one of his sons rushed into the house crying, "Paul is hurt! A car hit him and dragged him down the street! He was bleeding all over, and somebody came and took him away."

Vandall found his son at a nearby hospital with serious head injuries, a concussion, and multiple broken bones. The surgeon did not know if he would live. All the distraught father could do was pray as the doctor cleaned and stitched Paul's head wounds and set his broken bones. The rest was up to God.

After coming home to give his family the report, Vandall returned to the living room and fell on his knees with a heartfelt cry of, "Oh, God!" Almost immediately, Vandall could hear God's voice inside him, telling him that no matter what happened in the here and now, all tears will be dried and sorrows will cease in the hereafter. Vandall went to the piano and in minutes wrote a hymn titled "After."

After the toil and the heat of the day,
After my troubles are past,
After the sorrows are taken away,
I shall see Jesus at last.
He will be waiting for me –
Jesus so kind and true;
On His beautiful throne,
He will welcome me home –
After the day is through.

Paul had a near perfect recovery from his injuries, and his fathers faith in God remained strong and steady, his gratitude boundless.[13]

God wants to be with you in the midst of your tribulations too, putting a song of praise in your mouth. When you turn your focus from your struggles to Him, His awesome power can overcome whatever you are facing.

Tightrope Trust

I know whom I have believed, and am persuaded that he is able to keep that which I have committed unto him against that day.
2 TIMOTHY 1:12

In the mid-19th century, tightrope walker Blondin was going to perform his most daring feat yet. He stretched a two-inch steel cable across Niagara Falls. As he did, a large crowd gathered to watch. He asked the onlookers, "How many of you believe that I can carry the weight of a man on my shoulders across this gorge?"

The growing crowd shouted and cheered, believing that he could perform this difficult feat. Blondin picked up a sack of sand that weighed about 180 pounds and carried it across the Falls. They both arrived on the other side safely.

Then Blondin asked, "How many of you believe that I can actually carry a person across the gorge?" Again, the crowd cheered him on.

"Which one of you will climb on my shoulders and let me carry you across the Falls?" Silence fell across the crowd. Everyone wanted to see Blondin carry a person across the gorge, but nobody wanted to put his life into Blondin's hands.

Finally, a volunteer came forward willing to participate in this death-defying stunt. Who was this person? It was Blondin's manager, who had known the tightrope walker personally for many years.

As they prepared to cross the Falls, Blondin instructed his manager, "You must not trust your own feelings, but mine. You will feel like turning when we don't need to turn. And if you trust your feelings, we will both fall. You must become part of me." The two made it across to the other side safely.[14]

Jesus gives us the same instruction when we are asked to trust Him in difficult circumstances: "Don't trust your own feelings, trust Me to carry you through."

Fragments

*One day Jesus was praying in a certain place. When he fin-
ished, one of his disciples said to him, Lord teach us to pray.*
LUKE 11:1 NIV

Margaret Brownley tells of her son's first letters from camp: "When my oldest son went away to summer camp for the first time, I was a nervous wreck. Although he was nine years old, he hadn't as much as spent a night away from home, let alone an entire week. I packed his suitcase with special care, making sure he had enough socks and underwear to see him through the week. I also packed stationery and stamps so he could write home.

"I received the first letter from him three days after he left for camp. I quickly tore open the envelope and stared at the childish scrawl, which read: *Camp is fun, hut the food is yucky!* The next letter offered little more: *Jerry wet the bed.* 'Who's Jerry?' I wondered. The third and final letter had this interesting piece of news: *The nurse said it's not broken.*

"Fragments. Bits of information that barely skim the surface. A preview of coming attractions that never materialize. It made me think of my own sparse messages to God. 'Dear Lord,' I plead when a son is late coming home, 'keep him safe.' Or, 'Give me strength,' I pray when faced with a difficult neighbor or the challenge of a checkbook run amuck. 'Let me have wisdom,' is another favorite prayer of mine, usually murmured in haste while waiting my turn at a parent/teacher conference or dealing with a difficult employee. 'Thank-you, God,' I say before each meal or when my brood is tucked in safely for the night.

"Fragments. Bits and pieces. Are my messages to God as unsatisfactory to Him as my son's letters were to me? With a guilty start, I realized that it had been a long time since I'd had a meaningful chat with the Lord.

"When my son came home, he told me all about his adventures. It was good to have him home and safe. 'Thank you, God,' I murmured, and then caught myself. It was time I sent God more than just a hasty note from 'camp.'"[15]

Uniquely Fashioned

I will praise thee; for I am fearfully and wonderfully made;
marvelous are they works; and that my soul knoweth right
well.
PSALM 139:14

As you lie in bed tonight, stretch your limbs in all directions and then relax for a moment to ponder the fact that your body has been fearfully and wonderfully made. The word "fearfully" in this context is like the word of supreme quality that has been popular among teens in recent years, "Awesome!"

When you stop to think about all the intricate details involved in the normal functioning of your body —just one creation among countless species and organisms on the planet—you must conclude, "The Designer of *this* piece of work had a marvelous plan."

Listen to your heartbeat. Flex your fingers and toes. Keep in mind as you do that:

- no one else among all humanity has your exact fingerprints, hand print, or footprint,
- no one else has your voiceprint,
- no one else has your genetic code — the exact positioning of the many genes that define your physical characteristics.

Furthermore, nobody else has your exact history in time and space. Nobody else has gone where you've gone, done what you've done, said what you've said, or created what you have created. You are truly a one-of-a-kind masterpiece.

The Lord knows precisely *how* you were made and *why* you were made. When something in your life goes amiss, He knows how to fix it. When you err or stray from His commandments, He knows how to woo you back and work even the worst tragedies and mistakes for your good when you repent.

You have been uniquely fashioned for a specific purpose on the earth. He has a "design" for your life. It is His own imprint, His own mark. Make a resolution in these night hours to be true to what the Lord has made you to be and to become.

Heart's Home

Lord, thou hast been our dwelling place in all generations.
P S A L M   9 0 : 1

Thoughts of "Home Sweet Home" don't usu-ally conjure up high-tech images in our mind. But the new house of Microsoft CEO Bill Gates will have, not surprisingly, the latest in tech-nological comforts and conveniences. When you enter his new house you will receive an electronic pin to clip to your clothes. The pin identifies who and where you are and is programmed with your interests and tastes.

As you walk from room to room, the house adapts itself to your likes and dislikes. The temperature in each room automatically adjusts to your preference. The music you like will move with you from room to room. Digital images you want to see will appear on the walls of the rooms just before you enter and vanish after you leave.

What happens if there is more than one person in the room? No problem! The computer selects pro-gramming that suits both of your tastes![16]

Technology being what it is, someday we may all be able to customize our homes to respond to our most immediate interests, tastes, and comfort levels.

But there is something about the idea of "home" that goes well beyond the comfort and beauty of the physical surroundings. Home is a place where we can be ourselves. In that sense, there is a way in which no place on this planet will ever really be home for us.

George MacDonald in his work, *Thomas Wingfold, Curate,* said: "But there is that in us which is not at home in this world, which I believe holds secret relations with every star, or perhaps rather, with that in the heart of God whence issued every star . . . To that in us, this world is so far strange and unnatural and unfitting, and we need a yet homelier home. Yea, no home at last will do, but the home of Gods heart."

My Kingdom for Some Sleep

Let us draw near to God with a sincere heart in full assurance of faith, having our hearts sprinkled to cleanse us from a guilty conscience.
HEBREWS 10:22 NIV

In the recent past, the Internal Revenue Service received an envelope with one hundred $100 bills in it—no name, no address, no note—just money. Someone was feeling guilty.

On another day, the IRS received a large box containing a stack of handmade quilts. The note said, "Please sell these and use the money to settle my tax bill." Since the IRS isn't in the business of selling craft items, the quilts had to be returned.

One man believed he owed the US District Court $15.43. The court case in question had been held 18 years earlier, and the man just couldn't wrestle with his conscience any longer. The court insisted that the man didn't owe the money, but he refused to take no for an answer.

Another woman wrote to the IRS and said she felt guilty about cheating on her taxes; enclosed was a check. "If I still can't sleep," she said, "I'll send more."

The Bible has much to say about the blessings of a clear conscience and the agony of a guilty one. Perhaps the best example of a man who paid heed to his conscience was David. He made many mistakes, but he always admitted it when he did wrong. He was a man who couldn't sleep until he made peace with his Maker.

"For I know my transgressions, and my sin is always before me," he said. "Against you, you only, have I sinned and done what is evil in your sight, so that you are proved right when you speak and justified when you judge" (Psalm 51:4 NIV).

Are we as honest about our shortcomings as David was?

Confessing our sins brings release from guilt, peace of mind, and sweet sleep. As you retire for the night, check your heart. If you find any unconfessed sin, ask the Lord for forgiveness and He will give it. He is faithful and just to forgive you from your sins, and He will cleanse you from all unrighteousness. (See 1 John 1:9.)

Deal With It!

Be ye angry, and sin not: let not the sun go down upon your wrath.
E P H E S I A N S   4 : 2 6   K J V

One of the most controversial events in America occurred when Bernard Goetz had had enough and decided he wasn't going to take it any more. He did what many people have wanted to do —he fought back and pulled a gun when he was attacked on the subway.

Goetz' action received an outpouring of support. He touched a nerve in people who have simply had enough of other people threatening their lives. Criticism comes, however, when we allow guns in the hands of angry, violent people. As Christians, anger can be a terrible enemy.

The beginnings of anger almost go unnoticed: petty irritations, ordinary frustrations, minor aggravations—things we experience daily. Then these small things start adding up. Pressures build and turn into rage. Without relief, pent-up anger can turn violent, with devastating consequences.

How do we keep our passions from becoming uncontrolled anger? How should we defuse the anger that makes us want to retaliate?

There is a righteous, godly anger that energizes us to action, to right the wrong, to defend the innocent. However, anger becomes sin when it turns to hate and retribution. Then it is often expressed in inappropriate, destructive ways. We can fly off the handle and act in ways that are as hurtful as what caused us to be angry in the first place. Worse yet, we can store up anger and become bitter and resentful.

An old proverb says, "He who goes angry to bed has the devil for a bedfellow." This is not a condition for sweet sleep!

There are several things we can do to take control of our anger before it takes control of us:

1. Yell at God first! He already knows you're upset.

2. Ask God to give you understanding about the situation, to show you the root of your anger, if that's the case.

3. Turn the situation over to God. Forgive those who have hurt you and let Him deal with them. Turn His power loose in the circumstances.

4. Don't do anything without having complete inner peace from His Spirit.

Then you can sleep easily at night, knowing God can turn anything around to work for your good.

All the Details

Do not let your hearts be troubled. Trust in God; trust also in me.
JOHN 14:1 NIV

Andrea was in no mood for her six-year-old son's Saturday morning antics. While Steven argued with his friends over video games, Andrea stewed over her own mounting pile of pressures. Just-bought groceries for tomorrow's dinner guests sprawled across every bit of counter space. Buried under them was a Sunday school lesson to be prepared. A week's worth of laundry spilled out of the laundry room into the kitchen, and an upsetting letter from a faraway friend in need lay teetering on the edge of the sink.

In the midst of this turmoil, Steven's Sunday school teacher called. "Is Steven going to the carnival with us this afternoon?"

"He didn't mention anything about it."

"Well, we'll be leaving about noon. If he didn't bring home his permission slip, just write the usual information on a slip of paper and send it along with him." As soon as Andrea reminded Steven about the trip, his mood changed and he was his "better self" for the next couple of hours.

Andrea was just pulling a cake from the oven when she heard the doorbell ring, followed by an awful commotion. Rushing to the living room she found two little girls waving pink slips of paper at her crying son. "What's the matter?" she asked as she gently put her arms around him.

"I can't go!" he wailed. "I don't have one of those pink papers!"

"Oh, yes you do. Only yours happens to be white," she said as she dried his tears, stuffed the paper in his pocket, and sent him out the door.

Back in the kitchen Andrea wondered, "Why didn't he just ask me about the paper? Hasn't he been my child long enough to know I'd have a solution?"

Suddenly a tiny smile crept across her face as she surveyed the chaos around her—and she could almost hear her heavenly Father say, "Haven't you been My child long enough to know that I have it taken care of?"[17]

Calming Down

My sleep had been pleasant to me.
JEREMIAH 31:26 NIV

I t's virtually impossible for you to sleep if you are "wound up." Do memories of the day's events keep you from falling asleep? Do you sometimes feel as if you spent the day pushing a boulder up a mountain with a very small stick? Memorize these words:

I lift up my eyes to the hills — where does my help come from?
My help comes from the Lord, the Maker of heaven and earth.
PSALM 121:1-2 NIV

Are you worried about making mistakes, disappointing your boss, or letting your family down? Memorize these words:

He will not let your foot slip — he who watches over you will
not slumber; indeed, he who watches over Israel will neither
slumber nor sleep.
PSALM 121:3-4 NIV

Does unnecessary anxiety sometimes get the best of you, causing you to fear for your own safety or health? Memorize these words:

The Lord watches over you – the Lord is your shade at your right hand; the sun will not harm you by day, nor the moon by night.

PSALM 121:5-6 NIV

Are you already starting to agonize over next month's deadline, next year's taxes, the college tuition that has to be paid ten years from now, or funding your own retirement in thirty years? Are you taking all of that on when your head hits the pillow at night? Memorize these words:

The Lord will keep you from all harm – he will watch over your life; the Lord will watch over your coming and going both now and forevermore.

PSALM 121:7-8 NIV

You have just memorized an entire psalm! Repeat it to yourself every night. Substitute "my" for "your" and "me" for "you." Then rest in the knowledge that God has you, your life, and the rest of the universe under control.

Uniquely Positioned

*When I consider your heavens, the work of your fingers, the
moon and the stars, which you have set in place, what is man
that you are mindful of him?*
PSALM 8:3-4

A number of years ago, IMAX filmmakers produced a movie titled *Cosmos*. In it, they explored the "edges" of creation—both outer space as viewed through the most powerful telescope, and inner space as viewed through the most powerful microscope. Viewers saw for themselves that at the far reaches of space, clumps of matter (huge stars) seem to be suspended in fixed motion and separated by vast areas of seemingly empty blackness.

They also saw that the same can be said for the depths of inner space—clumps of matter are suspended in fixed orbits, separated by vast areas of seemingly empty blackness. In fact, the world of the distant stars is almost identical in appearance and form to the world of the tiniest neutrinos! Furthermore, neither of these "edges" of creation has been explored fully. Both inner and outer space appear as if they may very well extend into infinity.

In sharp contrast, the created earth as we experience it daily is uniquely suspended between these two opposite poles. Our world is filled with varied colors, dynamic forms, differing patterns, changing seasons, and adaptable functions.

It is as if God has placed man at the very center of His vast creation, with the maximum amount of complexity, meaning, and choice. We are "hung in the balances" literally, as well as figuratively — the pivot point between the great and the small, the vastness of outer space and the vastness of inner space.

We are not only fearfully and wonderfully made, but we are fearfully and wonderfully *positioned* in God's creation. The Lord has a place for mankind and specifically, He has a place for you. Thank God for your uniqueness today. Delight in all that makes you special in His eyes. Praise Him for all that He has designed you to be, to become, and to give.

Age is an Attitude

The righteous flourish like the palm tree . . . They still bring forth fruit in old age.
PSALM 92:12,14 RSV

Helen Keller was once asked how she would approach old age. She responded:

"Age seems to be only another physical handicap, and it excites no dread in me. Once I had a dear friend of eighty, who impressed upon me the fact that he enjoyed life more than he had done at twenty-five. 'Never count how many years you have, as the French say,' he would insist, 'but how many interests you have. Do not stale your days by taking for granted the people about you, or the things which make up your environment, and you will ever abide in a realm of fadeless beauty.'

"It is as natural for me, certainly, to believe that the richest harvest of happiness comes with age as that true sight and hearing are within, not without. Confidently I climb the broad stairway that love and faith have built to heights where I shall 'attain to a boundless reach of sky,'"[18]

The poem "How Old Are You?" reinforces this idea that *outlook* is what determines our age:

Age is a quality of mind:
If you have left your dream behind,
If hope is cold,
If you no longer look ahead,
If your ambition fires are dead —
Then you are old.
But if from life you take the best,
And if in life you keep the jest,
If love you hold;
No matter how the years go by,
No matter how the birthdays fly,
You are not old.[19]

Years before we reach what we would call "old age" we determine whether that time will be a gracious and pleasant time or a time when we rehearse life's hurts with bitterness. The attitudes with which we invest our days now will characterize the days of our senior years.

Not Exactly Puppy Love

But I say unto you, love your enemies.
MATTHEW 5:44

Aaron and Abbey had been happily married for nearly a year when Aaron bought Abbey a "present" she never wanted: a great big Chow puppy with paws the size of baseballs.

"Aaron, darling," Abbey said with conviction, "dogs and I are natural enemies. We just don't get along!"

"But Abs!" Aaron used his pet name for her hoping to soften her up, "You'll get used to him." It was pretty clear to them that the puppy was really a present for Aaron.

"Pup," as he came to be called, won an uneasy spot in their household. Determined that the dog should understand his place as her enemy, Abbey silently launched a campaign against him.

Pup sensed her resistance and reciprocated for a while by stealing towels, tearing up shoes and furniture, and carrying off whatever small object Abbey was using the minute she turned away. He completely ignored her attempts to correct him. So went Pup's first year in the family.

Then one day Abbey noticed a change in Pup's approach. To her astonishment, he began greeting her joyously each time she came home, nudging her hand and licking her fingers in a friendly "hello." Whenever she had to feed him he sat for a moment and gazed at her adoringly before he began eating. To top it off, he began accompanying her on her early morning walks, staying close at her side to ward off other dogs as she walked down their deserted road.

Little by little, Pup loved Abbey into a humbling truce. Today, Abbey says that Pup's persistence has taught her a lot about loving her enemies. She says Pup is winning—but don't tell Aaron.[20]

Is there someone you know—perhaps even someone in your own family—who needs an expression of your love, rather than your resistance?

Wild Passion Waves

Casting down imaginations, and every high thing that exalteth itself against the knowledge of God, and bringing into captivity every thought to the obedience of Christ.
2 CORINTHIANS 10:5

Eighteenth-century American poet Fitz-Greene Flalleck wrote: "There is an evening twilight of the heart, when its wild passion waves are lulled to rest." How many people long for that moment to come!

For millions of people, the last thoughts of the day are: "How can I get that thing or person I want?" "How might I further my own position in this life and capture the success that seems to elude me?" "How can I overcome my enemy and defeat my adversary?"

According to the apostle John, such thoughts are "lust of the flesh, and the lust of the eyes, and the pride of life" (1 John 2:16). Such desires can grow in our minds and hearts until they fill every waking moment. At that level of intensity, they defy sleep, for they require work . . . our work, our planning, our diligence, our decisions, our effort . . . in order to bring about a reward that is "our reward," the only kind satisfying to our pride.

How might these "wild passion waves" be lulled to rest? John offers the solution: Choose to be impassioned about something else, something eternal. "Love not the world . . . the world passeth away, and the lust thereof: but he that doeth the will of God abideth for ever" (1 John 2:15,17). Choose to "take captive" your thoughts and turn them toward what is eternal and eternally rewarding. If you are going to stay awake in your desire for something, make it a desire for the things of the Lord!

Choose to think about what you might do to further the Lord's kingdom—for example, a letter you might write to a prisoner, a gift you might give to a person in need, an act of kindness you might render to an elderly friend, a word of encouragement you might give to a child or teenager. As one preacher said, "Rather than count sheep, count the many ways the Lamb—Jesus Christ—desires for us to love His sheep! The devil will let you go to sleep right away!"

What Would You Say?

You are the salt of the earth . . . You are the light of the world.
MATTHEW 5:13-14 RSV

S tanding in line with his squad in the Red Army, Taavi had already made up his mind what he was going to say. The officers made their way toward him, interrogating each soldier down the line with the same question: "Are you a Christian?" "No," came the answer back. Then to the next one: "Are you a Christian?" "No," was the response.

The young conscripts stood at attention, their eyes fixed ahead. The questioners got closer to the 18-year-old Estonian who had been drafted into the Red Army during the Soviet occupation of his country.

Taavi had long been a Christian. Although only the older people were permitted to go to church in his country, Taavi's grandmother had shared her faith with her young grandson. He had accepted the Lord as his

Savior, and although he wasn't allowed to attend church, his grandmother taught him what she had learned each week.

The questioners neared. Taavi never really had any doubt what answer he would give. His mind had been made up years before, but he was still nervous. When the officers reached his place in line, they asked, "Are you a Christian?" Without flinching, Taavi said in a clear voice, "Yes."

"Then come with us," ordered the commanding officers.

Taavi followed them immediately. They got in a vehicle and drove to the building that housed the kitchen and mess hall. Taavi had no idea what was about to transpire, but he obeyed their orders.

The officers said to him, "We are taking you out of combat preparation. You are a Christian and you will not steal, so we will put you in the kitchen." The kitchen was the biggest black-market operation in the Red Army, with the smuggling and illegal sale of food to hungry soldiers. They knew Taavi's presence would reduce the amount of theft.

When you are challenged for your faith, rise up and boldly proclaim the truth. God will be with you, and He will reward you for your faithfulness.

A Dream So Fair

*And showed me the Holy City, Jerusalem, coming down out
of heaven from God.*
REVELATION 21:10 NIV

Thirty men, red-eyed and disheveled, lined
up before a judge of the San Francisco police
court. It was the regular morning company
of "drunks and disorderlies." Some were old and hard-
ened, others hung their heads in shame. The momen-
tary disorder that accompanied the bringing in of the
prisoners quieted down, and in that moment of calm, a
strange thing happened. A strong, clear voice from be-
low began singing: "Last night I lay a sleeping; there
came a dream so fair . . ."

Last night! It had been a nightmare or a drunken
stupor for them all. The song spoke of a contrast that
was sharp and convicting: "I stood in old Jerusalem,
beside the Temple there."

The song continued. The judge paused. He made a
quiet inquiry. A former member of a famous opera

company known throughout the nation was awaiting trial for forgery. It was he who was singing in his cell.

Meanwhile the song went on, and every man in the line showed emotion. One or two dropped on their knees; one boy sobbed, "Oh, mother, mother!"

The sobs could be heard from every corner of the courtroom. At length one man protested, "Judge," said he, "have we got to submit to this? We're here to take our punishment, but this . . ." He, too, began to sob. It was impossible to proceed with the business of court, yet the judge gave no order to stop the song: "Jerusalem, Jerusalem! Sing for the night is o'er! Hosanna in the highest!"

In an ecstasy of melody the last words rang out, and then there was silence. The judge looked into the faces of the men before him. There was not one who was not touched by the song; not one in whom some better impulse was not stirred.

He did not call the cases singly—he gave a kind word of advice and then dismissed them all. No man was fined or sentenced to the workhouse that morning. The song had done more good than punishment could possibly have accomplished.

The Day's Accomplishments

For in him we live, and move, and have our being.
A C T S   1 7 : 2 8

I f asked whether it's better to be proud or humble, most people would say "humble," since we have been taught that pride is a sin. However, if we think being humble means we are to denigrate ourselves or settle for mediocrity, we have the wrong definition of humility.

Humility is remaining teachable in all situations, knowing God is so much greater and we have so much to learn. Humility comes when we recognize God loves us just the way we are, that He will be patient as we strive to become like Him in character and word and deed.

Motivational speaker and author Denis Waitley has written:

"When you come down to the bottom line, joy is accepting yourself as you are right now — an imperfect, changing, growing, and worthwhile person. Realize that liking yourself and feeling that you're an OK individual in your own special way is not necessarily egotistical. Take pride in what you are accomplishing, and even more importantly, enjoy the unique person you are just in being alive right now. Understand the truth that although we as individuals are not born with equal physical and mental attributes, we are born with equal rights to feel the excitement and joy in believing we deserve the very best in life. "[21]

If you scored a victory today, if you won the prize, if you did the right thing, if you moved beyond yourself and extended an act of love and charity to another human being, rejoice in it! Delight in your awareness that the Lord is working in your life and *through* your life.

To delight in the Lord's work isn't pride. It's a form of praise to your Father, who is *proud* of you any time you succeed according to His principles and design. All the glory goes to Him. It is *because* of Him that we can succeed.

Heaven's Spot Remover

It is of the Lord's mercies that we are not consumed, because his compassions fail not. They are new every morning: great is thy faithfulness.
LAMENTATIONS 3:22-23

"Let it snow, let it snow, let it snow." That's the cry of school-aged children everywhere when winter weather finally arrives.

First, there's catching those early snowflakes on your tongue. After a few more flakes hit the ground, you can start making snowballs and have some terrific battles. Several inches later, it's time to build the snowmen and snow forts. And when the blanket of snow reaches a hefty thickness, the best thing to do is make snow angels.

Remember snow angels? You find a good patch of untouched snow, stand with your arms stretched out to the side, and fall backwards onto what feels like a cold, wet cloud. Stay on your back for a few moments and stare at the sky. When the cold starts getting to you, flap your arms and legs as if you're doing jumping jacks. Then, carefully get up and look at your handiwork.

Between the snowballs and snowmen, the forts and the angels, it isn't long before every square inch of clean snow has been used up. Patches of dead grass show through where someone dug down deep to roll a snowman's head. The once-pristine landscape is now trampled and rutted.

But something magical happens overnight. While you are sleeping, the snow falls again. You look out your window in the morning to find another clean white blanket covering all of the previous day's blemishes. All that was ugly is once again beautiful.

Don't despair when what began as a beautiful day turns into something ugly. Even though our own efforts to "fix it up" or "clean it up" might be futile, it can still be redeemed. The God who turned the humiliation and shame of His Son's death on the cross into the gift of salvation for all who believe in Him, can take the tattered rags of our daily lives and make them like new again—every morning.

Creator God

You are worthy, O Lord, to receive glory and honor and power; for You created all things, and by Your will they exist and were created.
R E V E L A T I O N 4 : 1 1 N K J V

When we see a beautiful piece of art or hear a stirring symphony, we ask, "Who is the artist? Who is the composer?" When we look at the wonders of nature we are often inspired in the same way, "How did this get here? Who made all this?"

W. Phillip Keller writes:

"It must be hard for skeptics, atheists, and agnostics to view sunrises and sunsets. The splendor of their glory, the beauty of their colors, the intensity of their inspiration that comes from the Fathers loving heart, are to the unbeliever nothing more than mere chemical and physical responses to external stimuli. No wonder their world is so bleak, their despair so deep, their future so forlorn."[22]

The writers of Scripture also saw God in His creation:

"The heavens declare the glory of God. "
PSALM 19:1 NKJV

"The earth shall be full of the knowledge of the Lord as the waters cover the sea. "
ISAIAH 11:9 NKJV

"God . . . rides through the heavens to your help, and in his majesty through the skies. "
DEUTERONOMY 33:26 RSV

"Since the creation of the world His invisible attributes are clearly seen."
ROMANS 1:20 NKJV

"The morning stars sang together and all the sons of God shouted for joy."
JOB 38:7 NKJV

Can you see God in the world around you? How big is He to you?

After Darkness, Dawn

But you are a chosen people, a royal priesthood, a holy na-
tion, a people belonging to God, that you may declare the
praises of him who called you out of darkness into his won-
derful light.
1 PETER 2:9 NIV

At the turn of the century there was a city worker whose youth had been spent in evil ways. But one night during a revival meeting he was spiritually born anew. Soon after, he ran into one of his old drinking pals. Knowing his friend needed Jesus, he attempted to witness to him about his newly found peace. His friend rebuffed him rudely and made fun of him for "turning pious."

"I'll tell you what," said the new Christian, "you know that I am the city lamplighter. When I go 'round turning out the lights, I look back, and all the road over which I've been walking is blackness. That's what my past is like."

He went on, "I look on in front, and there's a long row of twinkling lights to guide me, and that's what the future is like since I found Jesus."

"Yes," says the friend, "but by-and-by you get to the last lamp and turn it out, and where are you then?"

"Then," said the Christian, "why, when the last lamp goes out it's dawn, and there ain't no need for lamps when the morning comes."

Many children carry their fear of the dark into adulthood in the form of other kinds of fears. Fear of failure, rejection, loss, pain, loneliness, or disappointment. Each of these fears seems to grow in darkness. Darkness is a metaphor for many things: death, night, uncertainty, evil—but in all of them, Jesus is the Light that brings illumination and comfort.

When light shines, not only is darkness eliminated, but fears are relieved. Indeed, not only does Jesus give you as much light as you need to proceed in faith, but because of His sacrifice at Calvary, you can be assured of His eternal dawn when the last lamp goes out! Like the lamplighter said, "And there ain't no need for lamps when the morning comes."

Reviewing the Day

This I recall to my mind, therefore have I hope. It is of the Lord's mercies that we are not consumed, because his compassions fail not.
LAMENTATIONS 3:21-22

In *You Don't Have to Be Blind to See*, Jim Stovall writes:

"Your values determine your character, and they set a framework for the choices you make as well as a framework for evaluating your success. In other words, your values provide the framework for self-accountability . . .

Each night before I go to bed, I review the day I've just lived. And I evaluate it. I say about various things I've done or said, and about the choices I've made, 'That was good. That was great. That wasn't so hot.' In appraising my actions and decisions, I'm about to make midcourse corrections as I pursue my goals. In appraising my deeds of a day, I can close my eyes and have a sense of accomplishment, of being one step closer to the fulfillment of my destiny on earth."[23]

Reviewing the day and your values against the criteria of God's Word is a valuable exercise. It allows you to eliminate regret and pride, and you can wipe the slate clean for tomorrow's divine handwriting.

When you recall things about which you have remorse or sorrow, ask the Lord to forgive you for your sin, give you strength to turn from it, compensate for your errors, and help you to make amends wherever possible.

When you recall things about which you are pleased, give praise to the Lord for the wisdom, strength, and ability He provided throughout the day. Ask Him to use your "good deeds" and "right judgments" to expand His kingdom on the earth.

Before bed, put both good and bad in God's hands. You can rest in hope for tomorrow, because His mercy and compassion gives you a new opportunity to set things right, build on the good, and move forward in His power and love.

A Sabbath

But be glad and rejoice for ever in that which I create.
ISAIAH 65:18 RSV

What is it that gives you that warm fuzzy feeling inside? Certain smells, like the aroma of homemade bread right out of the oven or the cinnamon smell of hot apple cider, make you feel everything will be all right.

How about a crackling fire in the fireplace to chase away the damp chill on a rainy night? It makes you feel that life is good.

What about the whistling of a teakettle, ready to brew a pot of your favorite tea? Or listening to a favorite recording of Beethovens "Moonlight Sonata"? When was the last time you sat outside to do nothing else but watch the sun set?

To Oscar Hammerstein, that warm, fuzzy, everything-is-going-to-be-okay feeling came from "whiskers on kittens and warm, woolen mittens." What are some of *your* favorite things?

When was the last time you gave yourself permission to be "nonproductive" and enjoy some of life's simple pleasures?

Logan Pearsall Smith wrote, "If you are losing your leisure, look out! You may be losing your soul."

When we don't take time for leisure or relaxation, when we give our discretionary time away to busyness and relentless activity, we are living in a way that says, "everything depends upon me and my efforts."

Consequently, God prescribed a day of rest, the Sabbath, to enjoy His creation, to give us time to reflect and remember all He has done for us and all He is. The Sabbath is time to remember God is God—and we're not!

The Sabbath doesn't have to be Sunday. You can take a Sabbath rest anytime you relax and turn your focus to God and His creation. Sometimes you have nothing better to do than relax. You may have something *else* to do, but you don't have anything *better* to do.

Relax and just enjoy God's creation. After all, He *created* it for you to enjoy.

The Sunset Decision

*But if serving the Lord seems undesirable to you, then choose
for yourselves this day whom you will serve . . . But as for
me and my household, we will serve the Lord.*
JOSHUA 24:15 NIV

J enny Lind, known as "The Swedish Nightin-
gale," won worldwide success as a talented
opera singer. She sang for heads of state in
many nations and thrilled hundreds of thousands of people in an era when all performances were
live.

Not only did her fame grow, but her fortune in-
creased as well. Yet at the height of her career, at a time
when her voice was at its peak, she left the stage and
never returned.

She must have missed the fame, the money, and the
applause of thousands—or so her fans surmised—but
Jenny Lind was content to live in quiet seclusion with
her husband.

Once an English friend went to visit her. He found
her on the beach with a Bible on her knee. As he ap-

proached, he saw that her attention was fixed upon a magnificent sunset.

They talked of old days and former acquaintances, and eventually the conversation turned to her new life. "How is it that you came to abandon the stage at the apex of your career?"

Jenny offered a quiet answer that reflected her peace of heart: "When every day, it made me think less of this (laying a finger on the Bible) and nothing at all of that (pointing to the sunset), what else could I do?"

Has a busy, successful life robbed you of some of the most precious gifts of God? Next time you miss a sunset or prayer time because of a crowded schedule, remember Jenny's priorities.

Nothing in life is as precious as your relationship with your heavenly Father, and then your relationships with family members and friends. Ultimate fulfillment comes not in career or money, but in relationship with God and others.

Letting Go

Forgetting those things which are behind, and reaching forth
unto those things which are before, I press toward the mark
for the prize of the high calling of God in Christ Jesus.
PHILIPPIANS 3:13-14

The spider monkey is a tiny animal native to South and Central America. Quick as lightning, it is a very difficult animal to capture in the wild. For years, people attempted to shoot spider monkeys with tranquilizer guns or capture them with nets, but they discovered they were nearly always faster than their fastest draw or quickest trap.

Then somebody discovered the best method for capturing this elusive creature. They found that if you take a clear narrow-mouth glass bottle, put one peanut inside it, and wait, you can catch a spider monkey.

What happens? The spider monkey reaches into the bottle to get the peanut and he can't get his hand out of the bottle as long as it is clenching the peanut. The bottle is so heavy in proportion to his size, he can't drag it with him—and the spider monkey is too persistent to let go of a peanut once he has grasped it. In fact, you can dump a wheel barrow full of peanuts or bananas right next to him, and he won't let go of that one peanut.

How many of us are like that? Unwilling to change a habit, be a little flexible, try a new method, or give up something we know is bringing destruction to our lives? We stubbornly cling to *our way*, even if it brings pain and suffering.

Today, don't cling to a negative situation that may be draining you of your full vitality, energy, creativity, and enthusiasm for living. As the well-known phrase advises, "Let go, and let God!"

Trust the Lord to lead you to the wise counsel and new opportunities He has for you. Have faith in Him to provide what you truly need to live a peaceful, balanced, and fulfilling life. You may never lose your taste for peanuts, but with the Lord's help you can discern when they are trapped in glass bottles!

Solid Rock

See, I lay a stone in Zion, a tested stone, a precious corner-
stone for a sure foundation.
ISAIAH 28:16 NIV

Eighteenth-century hymn writer Edward Mote didn't know he needed God until he was sixteen years old. Apprenticed to a cabinetmaker, he went with his master to hear a great preacher and was immediately converted. He was God's man from that day forward, but it took him 55 years to realize one of his dreams: the building of a church for his local Baptist congregation.

Grateful to him for being the driving force behind the new building, the people offered him the deed to the property, which he turned down. All he wanted was the pulpit, to preach Jesus Christ. "When I stop doing that," he told them, "get rid of me!"

Of the more than 100 hymns he wrote, Mote is probably best known for "The Solid Rock." The chorus came to him one morning as he was preparing for work, and he had the first four verses written before the day was done. The following Sabbath, he stopped to visit a dying parishioner and sang the hymn to her. She was so comforted by it, her husband asked Mote to give him a copy. He did, but not before adding two more verses.

Struck by how much the song meant to the couple, Mote had a thousand copies of it printed and distributed. Today it remains one of the best-loved hymns of the church.

My hope is built on nothing less
Than Jesus' blood and righteousness;
I dare not trust the sweetest frame,
But wholly lean on Jesus' name.
On Christ, the solid Rock, I stand —
All other ground is sinking sand,
All other ground is sinking sand.[24]

All of us are building something on this earth, be it a relationship, a career, or a physical structure. Each day we are wise to check our foundation and make sure we're building on the Rock who will last forever.

Night Lights

You are my lamp, O Lord; the Lord turns my darkness into light.
2 SAMUEL 22:29 NIV

An Illinois pastor had six couples enrolled in a new-members class that met on Sunday evenings in one couple's home. Even after all the couples had completed the course work and joined the church, they continued to meet on Sunday evenings. They enjoyed each other's company and developed a deep sense of commitment to one another.

One night, the pastor received a call from one of the wives in the group. Her husband's plane had gone down, and she didn't know if he was dead or alive. The pastor immediately called the other group members, who rallied around her. They sat and prayed with her until word came that her husband was dead. Then various women took turns baby-sitting and staying with her during those first difficult nights.

Group members opened their homes to out-of-town relatives who came for the funeral. The men kept her car running and did yard work. And when she decided she would have to sell her house and find a smaller place to live, they helped her locate an apartment, pack, unpack, and settle into her new home.

For many people, this experience would seem like a night without end, a shadow on their lives that would never be erased. But because her friends let their lights shine into her darkness, they reminded her of the God who understood her pain and promised to see her through it.

"You are like light for the whole world," Jesus said. "A city built on top of a hill cannot be hidden, and no one would light a lamp and put it under a clay pot. A lamp is placed on a lamp stand, where it can give light to everyone in the house." (See Matthew 5:14-15.)

In a world that seems to grow darker day by day, let the Lord turn your darkness into light. Then you can brighten the lives of those around you by being one of Gods "night lights."

Running on Empty

There remains, then, a sabbath-rest for the people of God; for
anyone who enters God's rest also rests from his own work,
just as God did from his.
HEBREWS 4:9-10 NIV

S ome years ago, a research physician made an extensive study of the amount of oxygen a person needs throughout the day. He was able to demonstrate that the average workman breathes thirty ounces of oxygen during a day's work, but he uses thirty-one. At the close of the day he is one ounce short, and his body is tired.

He goes to sleep and breathes more oxygen than he uses to sleep, so in the morning he has regained five-sixths of the ounce he was short. The night's rest does not fully balance the day's work!

By the seventh day, he is six-sixths or one whole ounce in debt again. He must rest an entire day to re-plenish his body's oxygen requirements.

Further, he demonstrated that replenishing an en-tire ounce of oxygen requires thirty to thirty-six hours (one 24-hour day plus the preceding and following nights) when part of the resting is done while one is awake and moving about.

Over time, failure to replenish the oxygen supply results in the actual death of cells and, eventually, the premature death of the person.

A person is restored as long as he or she takes the seventh day as a day of rest.[25]

Sound familiar? The God who created us not only *invites* us to rest, He created our bodies in such a fashion that they *demand* rest.

Most people think that "keeping the Sabbath" is solely an act of devotion to God. But in turning your attention to Him, He can offer you true rest and replenishment in every area of your life—spirit, soul, *and* body. He is not only our daily strength, He is our source of rest, recreation, and replenishment.

———————————————————

Shalom

Peace I leave with you, my peace I give unto you.
JOHN 14:27

A word that appears throughout the Old Testament is "shalom." It is often translated "peace," but shalom means far more than peace in the aftermath of war or peace between enemies. Shalom embodies an inner peace which brings wholeness, unity, and balance to an individual's life. It describes a harmonious, nurturing environment which has God at its center.

In creation, God brought order and harmony out of chaos. He created shalom. It was man's sin that destroyed shalom, but it has always been God's plan that it be restored—first to the human heart, and flowing from that, heart-to-heart relationships.

In the book of Revelation, we have the glorious hope that the Prince of Peace will rule over a new heaven and earth that are described as perfect. According to Isaiah, justice, righteousness, and peace will characterize His unending kingdom. The Prince of Shalom will restore God's original shalom!

God has given us many promises for peace in His word. Meditate on His promises of shalom, and as you do, they will flood your heart and mind with peace, cleansing you from the stress of the day.

"Therefore, since we have been justified through faith, we have peace with God through our Lord Jesus Christ" (Romans 5:1 NIV).

"Great peace have they who love your law, and nothing can make them stumble" (Psalm 119:165 NIV).

"When a man's ways are pleasing to the Lord, he makes even his enemies live at peace with him" (Proverbs 16:7 NIV).

"May the God of hope fill you with all joy and peace as you trust in him, so that you may overflow with hope" (Romans 15:13 NIV).

"And the peace of God, which transcends all understanding, will guard your hearts and your minds in Christ Jesus" (Philippians 4:7 NIV).

You can have peace with God, peace in your walk, and peace with your enemies.

Shalom!

Looking Back

When you are on your beds, search your hearts and be silent.
PSALM 4:4 NIV

We all know the story of the movie *It's A Wonderful Life*. George Bailey's Uncle Billy loses $8,000 on the day the bank examiner shows up, and George is frantic. In despair, he goes home and looks at his house and family with discouraged eyes. He decides he is a failure at business, his child is sick, his house is all but coming down around his ears—why not just put an end to his life?

Thank God for Clarence! Through a series of events, this angel without wings shows George how much his life has meant to his family and friends. Without George, his brother Harry would be dead, Mr. Gower the druggist would be in prison, his wife would be a frightened old maid, and Bedford Falls would be known as Pottersville—a town as mean and miserable as its namesake.

When George Bailey took an honest look at his life, he could see that despite all the disappointments, there were more than enough triumphs to balance the scales. He had done the best he could, and that had brought tremendous blessing to his family, friends, and community.

At the end of the movie, George's brother calls him "the richest man in town" — and he was in all the ways that really matter.

Have you had a similar crisis of conscience, a moment when you wondered if your life was worth anything? Take note of these words from Bishop Thomas Wilson (1663-1755) and ask yourself these questions at the close of each day:

What good am I doing in the world?
Am I bringing up my children to fear God?
Have I been kind and helpful to poor and needy people?
Have I been honest in all my dealings?
Have I lived in the fear of God and worshipped Him both publicly and privately?[26]

The wisest thing to do is keep short accounts. Take stock of your life often. Don't wait for the closing chapter to decide how your book will end!

Five Minutes

In peace I will both lie down and sleep; for thou alone, O
Lord, makest me dwell in safety.
P S A L M   4 : 8   R S V

I f you wake up as weary as you were when you went to bed the night before, try to recall what you were thinking about the last five minutes before you went to sleep. What you think about in that five minutes impacts how well you sleep, which determines what kind of day tomorrow will be.

When you sleep, your conscious mind is at rest but your subconscious mind remains active. Psychologists call the subconscious the "assistant manager of life." When the conscious mind is "off duty," the subconscious mind takes over. The subconscious carries out the orders that are given to it, even though you are not aware of it.

For example, if the last minutes before going to sleep are spent in worry, the subconscious records and categorizes that as fear and acts as if the fear is reality. Thus muscles remain tense, nerves are on edge, and the body's organs are upset, which means the body is not really at rest.

However, if those last five minutes are spent contemplating some great idea, an inspiring verse, or a calm and reassuring thought, it will signal to the nervous system, "All is well," and put the entire body in a relaxed, peaceful state. This helps you to wake up refreshed, strengthened, and confident.

Many of the days that begin badly started out that way because of the night before, during those critical last five minutes of conscious thought. You can input positive, healthy thoughts into your conscious mind and pave the way for quiet, restful sleep by simply meditating on God's Word as you drop off to sleep. For example, Psalm 91:1-2 (NKJV):

"He who dwells in the secret place of the Most High shall abide under the shadow of the Almighty. I will say of the Lord, 'He is my refuge and my fortress; my God, in Him I will trust'."

Sweet dreams!

Serenity

I have [expectantly] trusted, leaned and relied on the Lord
without wavering, and I shall not slide.
PSALM 26:1 AMP

Many people are familiar with the "Serenity" prayer, although most probably think of it as a prayer to be said in the morning hours or during a time of crisis. Consider again the words of this prayer: "God grant me the Serenity to accept the things I cannot change, Courage to change the things I can, and Wisdom to know the difference."

Can there be any better prayer to say at the day's end? Those things which are irreversible or fixed in Gods order, we need to relinquish to Him. True peace of mind comes when we trust God knows more about any situation than we could possibly know. He can turn any situation from bad to good in His timing and according to His methods.

Those things we can change, we must have the courage to change. Furthermore, we must accept the fact that in most cases, we cannot change things until morning comes! We can rest in the interim, knowing the Lord will help us when the time comes for action.

The real heart of the Serenity prayer is revealed in its conclusion, that we might know the difference between what we need to accept and what we need to change. That takes wisdom. James tells us, "If any of you is deficient in wisdom, let him ask of the giving God [Who gives] to everyone liberally and ungrudgingly, without reproaching or faultfinding, and it will be given him. Only it must be in faith that he asks, with no wavering—no hesitating, no doubting" (James 1:5-6 AMP).

At day's end, we must recognize the Lord's wisdom may not be given to us *before* we sleep, but perhaps as we sleep, so that when we awaken, we have the answer we need. Many people have reported this to be true. They went to bed having a problem, turned it over to God in prayer, and awoke with a solution that seemed "plain as day" in the morning light.

Ask the Lord to give you true serenity tonight!

———————————

Print It!

Be very careful, then, how you live — not as unwise but as wise, making the most of every opportunity.
EPHESIANS 5:15-16 NIV

When we come to the end of the day and wonder why things went wrong, we usually don't have to look very far to discover the answer. Somehow, we lost our sense of direction and couldn't seem to get back on track. To ensure this doesn't happen again, or at least not as often, we can take some advice from *National Geographic* photographer Dewitt Jones.

Before he goes out to a shoot, Jones knows he has to have a good camera with the right lens. Different lenses give different perspectives. Jones experiments until he finds the right one.

1. If there's a problem at work that has you stymied, try looking at it from different points of view. Pray for "the eyes of your understanding to be enlightened." (See Ephesians 1:18.)

2. Another important factor is focus. With a turn of the lens, the whole picture can be razor sharp, or if Jones prefers, just the subject in the foreground will be clearly in focus.

3. We sometimes become so focused on one aspect of a problem, we lose sight of the big picture — of other circumstances influencing the situation or how the problem is going to affect others if it isn't resolved properly. Look at the big picture, then consider all individuals involved.

4. Jones allows his creative instincts to drive him to find more than one "right" way to shoot a photo. He uses about 400 rolls of film per article — and each published article uses approximately 50 photos.

5. Don't be afraid of experimenting with new ideas and methods. Ask God to show you "great and mighty things that you haven't known before." (See Jeremiah 33:3.) When Dewitt Jones empties his camera at the end of a shoot, he knows he's given it his best shot. He's looked at the subject he's photographing in as many different ways as he can think of.[27]

6. If we've found the right perspective, stayed focused on what's truly important, been willing to try something different, and refused to let fear of failure paralyze us, we too can look back at our day and say, "Print it!"

Night Light

In Him there is no darkness at all.
1 JOHN 1:5 NIV

A little boy was afraid to go to bed one night, because he couldn't see anything in the darkness. While his father was tucking him in, he said, "Do you love me when it's dark, Dad?"

"Of course, son."

"Do you love me even when you can't see me and I can't see you?"

"More than ever!"

Little children often need reassurance when the sun goes down, and sometimes adults do too. At night in the dark, worries seem to loom larger, problems greater, and fear stronger. This prayer can help put you at ease before going to sleep:

Lord Jesus, you are light from eternal lights.
You have dissolved all spiritual darkness
And my soul is filled with your brightness.
Your light makes all things beautiful.

You lit the skies with the sun and the moon.
You ordered night and day to follow each other peaceably.
And so you made the sun and the moon friends.
May I befriends with all whom I meet.

At night you give rest to our bodies.
By day you spur us on to work.
May I work with diligence and devotion,
That at night my conscience is at peace.

As I lay down on my bed at night,
May your fingers draw down my eyelids.
Lay your hand of blessing on my head
That righteous sleep may descend upon me.
        GREGORY OF NAZIANZUS [28]

Our heavenly Father loves us even in our dark times of worry and despair. His greatest desire in those times is for us to let the light of His Son Jesus light the darkness and dispel the shadows. Let Jesus be your night light tonight!

Heavenly Minded

For we are his workmanship, created in Christ Jesus for good works, which God prepared beforehand, that we should walk in them.
EPHESIANS 2:10 RSV

"If you read history you will find that the Christians who did most for the present world were just those who thought most of the next," wrote C. S. Lewis.

Recent research bears out this fact. Robert Wuthnow reports, "Christians are more likely to volunteer than other citizens, more prone to give significant time to caring for others, and more likely to believe that they have a duty to do so. Those who attend church regularly, who are active in fellowship and Bible-study groups, who gain a great deal of satisfaction from their religion are far more active volunteers than those who have little church involvement and gain little satisfaction from faith."

One reason why Christians are likely to be involved in helping others is they don't see their life on earth as the sum total of their existence. In fact, this life is simply an opportunity to do good.

Christians are actually citizens of another place—heaven. They are persons whose Father is in heaven; their treasure and home are in heaven. They are born from above and their affections and attention are set on things above. As citizens of heaven, they are ambassadors who represent the kingdom of heaven on earth.

What does it mean to be an ambassador?

• An ambassador is a representative.
• An ambassador is a foreigner in the country where they are living.
• An ambassador is only a temporary resident of the country where they are living.
• An ambassador always keeps in mind the one they serve; that is their purpose.
• An ambassador will assist those who wish to emigrate to their country.

Turn your thoughts toward heaven before sleeping tonight. See how it changes your perspective about your life on earth.

Endless Love

I have loved you with an everlasting love; I have drawn you
with lovingkindness.
JEREMIAH 31:3 NIV

The beautiful hymn, "O Love That Will Not Let Me Go," was penned by a Scottish minister, George Matheson, who was totally blind. While he would never disclose what triggered the beautiful lyrics, it was widely speculated his sister's wedding reminded him of a heartbreaking event. Just before he was to wed his college sweetheart, she was told of his impending blindness. She is said to have informed him, "I do not wish to be the wife of a blind preacher." Matheson gives this account:

"My hymn was composed . . . the night of my sister's marriage . . . Something happened to me, which was known only to myself, and which caused me the most severe mental suffering. The hymn was the fruit of that suffering. It was the quickest bit of work I ever did in my life. I had the im-

pression of having it dictated to me by some inward voice rather than of working it out myself."

Having experienced rejection from an earthly lover, Matheson wrote of a heavenly Lover whose love is eternal and faithful:

O love that wilt not let me go,
I rest my weary soul on Thee;
I give Thee back the life I owe,
that in Thine ocean depths its flow
may richer, fuller be.

O light that follow'st all my way,
I yield my flick'ring torch to Thee;
my heart restores its borrowed ray,
that in Thy sunshine's blaze
its day may brighter, fairer be.[29]

The love that first drew you to God is the same love that now surrounds you tonight and will be with you forever, in all situations. Whatever you are going through, allow Him to comfort you.

What Do You Want?

I thank You and praise You, O God of my fathers, Who has given me wisdom and might and has made known to me now what we desired of You.
DANIEL 2:23 AMP

Children are quick to respond to their environment. Babies immediately cry when they are hungry, thirsty, tired, sick, or wet. Toddlers are not at all bashful in communicating what they do and do not want.

However, as we grow older maturity teaches us to use discernment in making our desires known, that we give way to the needs of others in many situations.

The Lord nevertheless tells us we are wise to always come to Him as little children—telling Him precisely what we need and want. While looking directly at a man whom He knew was blind, Jesus asked him, "What do you want Me to do for you?" (Mark 10:51 AMP). Without hesitation he replied, "Master, let me receive my sight."

Jesus could see he was blind, yet He asked him to make a request. In like manner, God knows what you need "before you ask Him" (Matthew 6:8 AMP). Yet He says in His Word, "by prayer and petition [definite requests] . . . continue to make your wants known to God" (Philippians 4:6 AMP).

Why pray for what seems to be obvious? Because in stating precisely what we want, our needs and desires become obvious to *us*.

If we stop to listen to our own petitions, we come face to face with our priorities, our hurts, and our excesses. We see ourselves more clearly, and thus have an opportunity for repentance, to see the core of an issue—something we may have skirted or refused to handle. At other times, we know precisely where we need to take action or say to someone, "Enough is enough."

State your requests boldly before the Lord tonight. He'll hear you. He'll respond to you. And just as important, you'll hear yourself and respond in a new way to Him.

Shining Through

Let your light so shine before men, that they may see your
good works and glorify your Father in heaven.
MATTHEW 5:16 NKJV

A little girl was among a group of people being given a guided tour through a great cathedral. As the guide explained the various parts of the structure—the altar, the choir, the screen, and the nave, the little girl's attention was intently focused on a stained glass window.

For a long time she silently pondered the window. Looking up at the various figures, her face was bathed in a rainbow of color as the afternoon sun poured into the transept of the huge cathedral.

As the group was about to move on, she gathered enough courage to ask the tour conductor a question. "Who are those people in that pretty window?"

"Those are the saints," the guide replied.

That night, as the little girl was preparing for bed, she told her mother proudly: "I know who the saints are."

"Oh?" replied the mother. "And just who *are* the saints?"

Without a moments hesitation the little girl replied: "They are the people who let the light shine through!" [30]

As you look back over your day, did you let God's light shine through? Sometimes we pass these opportunities by saying, "It will just take too much out of me." But the Bible lets us know that everything we give will come back to us — multiplied. (See Luke 6:38.)

We see this principle in nature. A microscopic speck of radium can send out a stream of sparks which give off light and heat, yet in emitting the light and heat, it does not deplete itself of its own energy.

As Christians we are called to share the light of Jesus in a world of darkness. Like rays of light that break through gloom and darkness, we can bring hope and encouragement.

Remember, the light of your life gives those around you a glimpse of Jesus, the Source of eternal and constant light. As you let your light shine, it will grow brighter!

Beyond the Sunset

Now we see but a poor reflection as in a mirror; then we shall see face to face. Now I know in part; then shall I know fully, even as I am fully known.
1 CORINTHIANS 13:12 NIV

The ability to see "beyond the sunset" — to anticipate the glories of God's tomorrow — enables a Christian to live joyfully and victoriously in any of life's circumstances.

Virgil P. Brock told how he wrote the beloved hymn "Beyond the Sunset":

"This song was born during a conversation at the dimer table, one evening in 1936, after watching a very unusual sunset at Winona Lake, Indiana, with a blind guest, my cousin Horace Burr, and his wife, Grace. A large area of the water appeared ablaze with the glory of God, yet there were threatening storm clouds gathering overhead. Our blind guest excitedly remarked that he had never seen a more beautiful sunset.

"People are always amazed when you talk about seeing,' I told him. 'I can see,' Horace replied. 'I see through other people's eyes, and I think I often see more; I see beyond the sunset.'

"The phrase 'beyond the sunset' and the striking inflection of his voice struck me so forcibly, I began singing the first few measures. 'That's beautiful!' his wife interrupted. 'Please go to the piano and sing it.'

"We went to the piano nearby and completed the first verse. Before the evening meal was finished, all four stanzas had been written and we sang the entire song together."

The first verse of his beautiful hymn says:

Beyond the sunset, O blissful morning,
when with our Savior heav'n is begun.
Earth's toiling ended, O glorious dawning —
beyond the sunset when day is done.[31]

Fulfillment

I have come that they might have life, and that they might
have it more abundantly.
JOHN 10:10 NKJV

Fulfillment is something for which every person seems to long. In its simplest meaning, fulfillment refers to being "fully filled" — having a complete sense of accomplishment.

If you lack a sense of fulfillment at day's end, ask yourself, "What did I not do that I felt I should have done?" You'll be calling into question your values, priorities, and goals. As you see areas in which you have fallen short, ask the Lord to help you discipline yourself to achieve what you know is good, adjust your priorities and goals, and refine your values.

A lack of fulfillment isn't the fault of circumstances or another person's behavior. It is a matter of your outer life being in harmony with your inner life, living outwardly what you profess with your mouth and believe in your heart.

For Robert Louis Stevenson, this was the definition of a successful life:

"That man is a success who has lived well, laughed often and loved much; who has gained the respect of intelligent men and the love of children; who has filled his niche and accomplished his task; who leaves the world better than he found it, whether by an improved poppy, a perfect poem, or a rescued soul; who never lacked appreciation of earth's beauty or failed to express it; who looked for the best in others and gave the best he had."[32]

Do you have a definition of success against which to gauge your own sense of fulfillment?

There's still time to make today fulfilling. Take a moment to reflect upon your goals, priorities, and values. Ask the Lord to show you where they may need some adjusting. As you rethink these important issues you will be filled with the knowledge that true fulfillment comes in simply knowing and obeying Him.

———————————————

Reverence, Not Ritual

He said to them, "Why are you troubled, and why do doubts
rise in your minds."
LUKE 24:38 NIV

Have you ever met someone who, when something good comes their way, starts wondering when God is going to take it back?

Long ago, pagans in Germany and Holland believed this way. If Johann met Hans in the forest and said, "Hey Hans! I got that horse I wanted — good price, too!" in a second both men would gasp. Johann would run to the nearest tree and start pounding on it.

The pagans believed that the gods lived in trees, and if they heard about any human happiness, they would cause mischief. Johann, realizing his mistake in the listening forest, would rap on trees to drive the gods away. Even when it was no longer a custom to literally "knock on wood," the phrase sufficed to fill the same purpose: "May my good fortune suffer no reversal."

In our lives, it's either "Thy will be done" or "knock on wood." Either God is working for our good, or we must be working for our good.

How sad it must make our heavenly Father to see us robbed of joy as we receive His blessings, simply out of fear. Furthermore, some people feel the only way to hold onto the joys of life is to perform good deeds. They believe if they don't go through certain rituals in life, they risk losing things of value. As a result, those parts of the Christian life that should bring us closer to the heart of God often end up as rituals performed out of duty and fear.

When the city of Hamburg was stricken with the plague and large numbers were dying, the healthy—in mortal dread of becoming ill—flocked to the city's churches. It was not a reverence for God that drew them to church, but the fear of cholera. As soon as the plague abated, their zeal for the worship of God also abated.

The Ford desires an intimate, honest relationship with you—not a relationship rooted in your fear of loss or failure. The "fear of God" does not mean you're "afraid" of God, it means you have respect for God. This reverence is born out of trust in His love. Turn to Him this evening for life, not merely to avoid disaster. When you do, you'll meet a heavenly Father who loves you completely and unconditionally.

Like a Child

Truly I tell you, whoever does not receive and accept and welcome the kingdom of God like a little child [does] positively shall not enter it at all.
MARK 10:15 AMP

———————

Many a parent has stood in awe by the bed of their sleeping child, amazed at the miracle of his life, captured by his sweet expression of innocence, and bewildered by his ability to sleep peacefully regardless of the turmoil that may be around him.

Those same parents have also felt great frustration earlier in the day when their child was willful or disobedient, and they marveled at their child's ingenuity, energy, curiosity, or humor. Children seem to embody all of life's extremes.

What did Jesus mean when He said we must receive and welcome the kingdom of God as a little child? Surely He meant we must accept and embrace God's will for our lives with a sense that "this is what is and isn't it grand" —welcoming the Lord's will without debate, without question, without worry or fear, and with a sense of delight, expectation, and eagerness.

As a child opens a present, he has no doubt that the pretty paper and ribbon hides a happy surprise. In the same way, we must anticipate that the kingdom of God is a joyful and wonderful gift to us, one in which we can delight thoroughly.

Andrew Gillies has written a lovely poem to describe the childlikeness the Lord desires to see in us. Let it inspire your own prayer this evening:

Last night my little boy confessed to me
Some childish wrong;
And kneeling at my knee,
He prayed with tears —
"Dear God, make me a man like Daddy —
Wise and strong; I know you can!"

Then while he slept I knelt beside his bed,
Confessed my sins,
And prayed with low-bowed head —
"O God, make me a child like my child here —
Pure, guileless,
Trusting Thee with faith sincere."[33]

Think On These Things

But his delight is in the law of the Lord, and on his law he meditates day and night.
PSALM 1:2 NIV

———————————————

I n a recent study, twenty-two women experiencing "high-anxiety" were hooked up to heart monitors and told to spend ten minutes watching the beat of their pulses on special wristwatches. After twelve weeks of this, all of the women had definite improvement in their anxiety levels.

An additional thirty-three women were tested at the same time. Their anxiety-reducing exercise was reading magazines. Reading proved less effective than simply watching a pulse beat. What is it about taking ten minutes to watch your heartbeat that makes one less anxious?

One of the doctors involved in the study said that when you sit and focus on these steady rhythms, you are forced to remain in the moment. Dedicating yourself to this task for ten minutes takes your mind off both the past and the future—the two hobgoblins of modern life.

There are 960 working minutes in a day (if you allow eight hours for sleep). This doctor points out that all of us can find ten minutes for this simple form of "meditation"—especially when the payoff is less stress.[34]

In the Bible, God commanded Joshua to engage in a different kind of exercise: "Do not let this Book of the Law depart from your mouth; meditate on it day and night" (Joshua 1:8 NIV).

When Joshua meditated on Gods Word, he was focusing on something that would help him live a righteous life at that moment. Foremost in his mind was the question, "What does God want me to do right now? How can I keep my finger on God's pulse?"

As you lie in bed tonight, place your hand over your heart and feel the pulse of your physical life for a few minutes. Then turn your attention to the pulse of your spiritual life, Jesus Christ, who lives in your heart.

Ask Jesus what He would like you to be thinking about as you fall asleep.

A Hint of Eternity

We fix our eyes not on what is seen, but on what is unseen.
For what is seen is temporary, but what is unseen is eternal.
2 CORINTHIANS 4:18 NIV

———————

E ternity is a difficult concept for us to grasp. In human terms, it seems a matter of time — or more accurately, timelessness. But eternity is more than a measure of time. Things said to be "eternal" have a quality of permanence. The benefits of eternal things are not found solely in the hereafter; they provide an incredible sense of satisfaction in this life as well.

The late Lorado Taft, one of America's great artists, often said that a real work of art must have in it "a hint of eternity." The writer of Ecclesiastes says that God has not only made everything beautiful, but He has set eternity in the heart of man. (See Ecclesiastes 3:11 Niv.) When we do a good piece of work, whether it is part of our vocation or not, we may find in it a hint of eternity, the abiding value that outlasts silver or gold.

Daniel Webster, one of America's most famous statesmen, once said: "If we work on marble, it will perish; if on brass, time will efface it; if we rear temples, they will crumble into dust; but if we work on immortal souls and imbue them with principles, with the just fear of God and love of our fellowmen, we engrave on those tablets something that will brighten to all eternity."

Ascending to the top of one of the magnificent stairways in the Library of Congress, one reads this inscription on the wall: "Too low they build who build beneath the stars."

In building your life, build with God for eternity. In building the church, build to the glory of Jesus Christ for the salvation of souls.

Ask the Lord to show you this evening how to make your life and effort count for eternity. Pray for an awareness of eternity as you face every decision and task tomorrow.

Go Gently into the Night

He will feed His flock like a shepherd, He will gather the
lambs in His arms, He will carry them in His bosom, and
will gently lead those that have their young.
ISAIAH 40:11 AMP

"Gentleness" is a soothing, comforting word. It evokes thoughts of peace and rest. We long for a sense of this peace in our homes. We desire an uninterrupted time of relaxation before we retire. Bedtime beverages and conversations that are soothing and edifying, a night free of terrors, and dreams that are beautiful. We desire to be treated gently. Gentleness marks an environment we find comforting, uplifting, and calming.

Garrison Keillor described a gentle life in this way:

"What keeps our faith cheerful is the extreme persistence
of gentleness and humor. Gentleness is everywhere in daily
life, a sign that faith rules through ordinary things: through

cooking and small talk, through storytelling, making love, fishing, tending animals and sweet corn and flowers, through sports, music, and books, raising kids — all the places where the gravy soaks in and grace shines through. Even in a time of elephantine vanity and greed, one never has to look far to see the campfires of gentle people. Lacking any other purpose in life, it would be good enough to live for their sake."[35]

While gentleness is a quality of environment we desire, we must recognize that gentleness begins within the heart. Gentleness is described in the Scriptures as one of the "fruits of the Spirit" (Galatians 5:22-23).

Choose to deal with your family members and friends with gentleness this evening — with kindness, simplicity, and tenderness. In planting seeds of gentleness you will reap a gentle evening in which to relax, and find rest for your body, mind, and soul.

Vital Connections

As you received Christ Jesus the Lord, so continue to live in him. Keep your roots deep in him and have your lives built on him.
COLOSSIANS 2:6-7 NCV

T he root system of bunch grass that grows in the hilly high country is deep, far reaching, and very extensive. A single plant may have up to seventeen miles of roots growing underground. This sturdy grass withstands the extensive grazing and trampling of livestock and each year puts out new growth.

All year round the bunch grass provides protein for animals. Even when covered by winter snow, it provides rich nutrition for deer, mountain sheep, and range horses. In the fall, its bronze blades provide one of the best nutrition sources available.

People also need vast root systems so their lives can be nourished and provide nourishment for others. Our root system gives us the strength to withstand being "trampled" by the challenges we face everyday and the nutrition we need to replenish our resources when we've been "grazed" upon.

What makes up our root system? For most of us, it's family. Our parents and relatives began nurturing us the day we were born. No matter how many miles or years separate us, we turn to them (or to our memory of what they taught us) for wisdom and guidance.

Another part of our root system is people outside the family circle—our friends, coworkers, and people in our church, who have loved us, believed in us, and given us a helping hand as we've struggled to find our place in the world.

More important than all these is our vital connection to God. If your family, friends, coworkers, and church forsake you, God will never forsake you. He is the One Who knows everything about you and still loves you. He gives you the desires of your heart and has shaped your destiny.

Let your roots grow down deep into the soil of God's loving presence, and He will provide you with nourishment that will overflow into the lives of all those around you.

———————————————

Forty Winks

He who keeps you will not slumber. Behold, He who keeps
Israel shall neither slumber nor sleep.
P S A L M   1 2 1 : 3 - 4   N K J V

How can young doctors be on duty nearly 24 hours at a time, day after day, and still be alert in a crisis?

Belgian researchers decided to do a study of hospital residents and the effects of their grueling schedules. Stress levels were measured after residents worked a 24-hour shift that encompassed the emergency room, regular ward duties, and the intensive-care unit, followed by a return to the ward at the end of the shift.

Although lack of sleep played a part in raising levels of stress-related hormones, the researchers concluded that a heavy workload on top of important responsibilities was the foremost factor in creating stress. Another way of looking at the research is to say, it's still possible to do an excellent job, even when you're exhausted.

Have you ever tried to stay up for more than 24 hours? It's a near-impossible feat for most of us. Some scientists believe that sleep-inducing chemicals build up in the brain and eventually knock us out. But with certain jobs (such as being a physician) or round-the-clock responsibilities (such as parenting) some of us are occasionally called upon to pull double duty.

Rested or not, we have to be ready to jump into action at a moments notice. We can do it—especially if we've managed to keep our normal workload and responsibilities within bounds.

In a medical emergency, it takes several people to perform all the ministrations required, and it requires shift work to be sure everyone is rested enough to do their jobs well.[36]

In your times of need, be willing to ask others for help. And above all, seek the help of your heavenly Father, Who never sleeps. He is able to watch over you and provide for you every waking—and sleeping—moment.

_____

Discretionary Time

In all your getting, get understanding.
PROVERBS 4:7 NKJV

M odern time-saving appliances and devices give us the opportunity to make choices about how to use our time. We can spend less time doing things we don't enjoy in order to have more time to do the things we do enjoy. But what is it we enjoy doing?

Twenty-year-old college student Amy Wu wrote about her aunt who "tends to her house as if it were her child." The house is spotlessly clean. Smells of home-cooked meals drift through the house. Roses from the garden are artfully arranged in beautiful vases. Her aunt can afford a housekeeper, but she enjoys doing her own housework.

Amy went on, "I'm a failure at housework. I've chosen to be inept and unlearned at what my aunt has spent so much time perfecting. At 13, I avoided domestic chores as my contribution to the women's movement. Up to now, I've thought there were more important things to do."

But those "more important things" didn't turn out to be all that important. She explained, "It isn't as if we're using the time we save for worthwhile pursuits . . . Most of my friends spend the extra minutes watching TV, listening to stereos, shopping, hanging out, chatting on the phone, or snoozing."

One day she decided to make a meal for her family. While the dinner was cooking she wrote a letter to her cousin. Then she made a chocolate cake to celebrate her sister's birthday. It was a success: "That night I grinned as my father and sister dug into the pasta, then the cake, licking their lips in appreciation. It had been a long time since I'd felt so proud. A week later my cousin called and thanked me for my letter, the first handwritten correspondence she'd received in two years."

She concluded, "Sure, my generation has all the technological advances at our fingertips. We're computer-savvy, and we have more time. But what are we really saving it for? In the end, we may lose more than we've gained by forgetting the important things in life."[37]

How do you spend your discretionary time? Like Amy's friends, caring for family, growing closer to the Lord? In all your getting, get understanding!

Home Fires

Teach the young women to be sober, to love their husbands,
to love their children.
TITUS 2:4

E rnestine Schuman-Heink is not the first to ask, "What is a home?" But her answer is one of the most beautiful ever penned:

"A roof to keep out the rain. Four walls to keep out the wind. Floors to keep out the cold. Yes, but home is more than that. It is the laugh of a baby, the song of a mother, the strength of a father. Warmth of loving hearts, light from happy eyes, kindness, loyalty, comradeship. Home is first school and first church for young ones, where they learn what is right, what is good and what is kind. Where they go for comfort when they are hurt or sick. Where fathers and mothers are respected and loved. Where children are wanted. Where the simplest food is good enough for kings because it is earned. Where money is not so important as loving-kindness. Where even the tea-kettle sings from happiness. That is home. God bless it."[38]

God asks us to call Him "Father," and family life is at the heart of the Gospel. Through Jesus Christ, God the Father has forged a way to adopt many children. As a result, the Scriptures have much to say about what a happy home should be like. Good family life is never an accident, but an achievement by those who share it.

When our heavenly Father is the center of our homes, our homes will be a reflection of Him. But sometimes this is easier said than done. That's why He gave us 66 books of the Bible to help us! We must learn His way of thinking and doing things. Then we must teach our children what He teaches us.

Keeping the home fires burning is letting God's Word and presence guide your way and keeping the love of God ablaze in the hearts of your family.

The Dinner Table

And He took bread, gave thanks and broke it, and gave it to them.
LUKE 22:19 NKJV

In our modern society, with frantic schedules, fast-food restaurants, and microwave ovens, family members frequently "catch a meal" whenever and wherever they can, eating it "on the run."

Nevertheless, when we reflect upon the good times we have shared with family members, our memories often settle upon family meals—not necessarily holiday feasts, but daily family dinner conversation. When we sit at a table with one another, we not only share food, but our lives.

Elton Trueblood has written eloquently about family dinnertime. Perhaps it's time we reinstitute this practice in our lives!

"The table is really the family altar! Here those of all ages come together and help to sustain both their physical

and their spiritual existence. If a sacrament is 'an actual conveyance of spiritual meaning and power by a material process,' then a family meal can be a sacrament. It entwines the material and the spiritual in a remarkable way. The food, in and of itself, is purely physical, but it represents human service in its use. Here, at one common table, is the father who has earned, the mother who has prepared or planned, and the children who share, according to need, whatever their antecedent participation may have been."

When we realize how deeply a meal together can be a spiritual and regenerating experience, we can understand something of why our Lord, when he broke bread with his little company toward the end of their earthly fellowship, told them, as often as they did it, to remember him. We, too, seek to be members of his sacred fellowship, and irrespective of what we do about the Eucharist, there is no reason why each family meal should not take on something of the character of a time of memory and hope.[39]

When was the last time your family gathered together for a meal?

Fishing

Where the river flows everything will live.
EZEKIEL 47:9 NIV

O nce upon a time, fishing was a survival skill. If you wanted to eat, you learned how to fish. Much later it became a form of recreation. In modern times, it has become a sport, with fishermen competing to see who can catch the first fish, the largest fish, the orneriest fish, or the most fish.

For the purist, fishing is still a chance to commune with nature, to become one with the great outdoors. Let's face it: The first rule of fishing, when you're sitting in a boat in the middle of a lake, is to be quiet! Maybe you can bend this rule in the ocean, or while standing in a rushing stream with the water nearly topping your waders, but on a tranquil lake or pond, quiet is imperative.

For an avid fisherman, fishing does more than take him away from the noise and confusion of daily life. By just thinking back to previous fishing trips, he can momentarily escape his busy day and stuffy office.

He can remember the way the sunlight or moonlight looked when it hit the water, the sight of animals or insects going about their business and giving little or no thought to the human in their midst, the satisfaction that came from being alone but not lonely, and the times he chose to share his quiet retreats with one or two friends. Memories such as these are like a park bench in a grove of trees on a cool spring day, a place to lie down and take a deep breath.

In this figurative sense, all of us need a boat in the middle of the lake to escape to now and then. We need a place where we can sit down, throw our lines in the water, and wait patiently for the fish to bite. And if they aren't biting? Who cares? As any zealous fisherman will tell you, it's not always about filling your bucket. Sometimes, it's about enjoying the warm sun on your head, the wind in your face, and the peace that invades your soul.

Resting in the Lord

*He who dwells in the shelter of the Most High will rest in
the shadow of the Almighty.*
PSALM 91:1 NIV

There is a story about an English steamer
which was wrecked on a rocky coast many
years ago. Twelve women set out into the
dark stormy waters in a lifeboat and the boisterous sea
immediately carried them away from the wreckage.
Having no oars, they were at the mercy of the wind
and the waves. They spent a fearful night being tossed
about by the raging tempest.

They probably would have lost all hope if it had
not been for the spiritual stamina of one of the ladies,
who was well known for her work in sacred oratorios.
Calmly she prayed aloud for divine protection. Then,
urging her companions to put their trust in the Lord,
she encouraged them by singing hymns of comfort.

Throughout the dark hours her voice rang out
across the water. Early the next morning a small craft
came searching for survivors. The man at the helm

would have missed the women in the fog if he had not heard a woman singing the selection from *Elijah*. "Oh, rest in the Lord, wait patiently for Him!" Steering in the direction of her strong voice, he soon spotted the drifting lifeboat. While many others were lost that night, these trusting few were rescued.

Have you ever had a long sleepless night when the trials and "storms" of the day refused to leave you? Have you found yourself unable to sleep because of worries about what tomorrow may bring? Perhaps you have felt you were adrift in an ocean of responsibilities with no rescue in sight.

Instead of lying there awash in worry, frustration, fear, or anger, try singing hymns of faith—either aloud or silently—in your mind. As you turn your thoughts to the true Rescuer, you are likely to find yourself relaxing in His arms and drifting off to sweet sleep.

———————————

Fix Your Focus

"I know the plans I have for you," declares the Lord, "plans to prosper you and not to harm you, plans to give you hope and a future."
JEREMIAH 29:11 NIV

Danish philosopher Soren Kierkegaard addresses the nature of true humility by suggesting we think of an arrow soaring on its course toward its target. Suddenly the swift-moving arrow halts in mid-flight to see how far it has come, how high it has soared, how its speed compares with another arrow, or to apprehend the grace and ease with which it flies. Right at the moment when it turns to focus on itself, the arrow falls to the ground.

Preoccupation with self is counterproductive to reaching our goals. It is the opposite of humility, which is preoccupation with the Lord.

How many times do we compare ourselves to others and measure our success or failure according to someone else's life? The Bible says this is not wise. (See 2 Corinthians 10:12.) The reason God tells us that comparing ourselves to others is not wise is because His plan for our life is totally unique. If we have a question about our life, we should look to Him.

As for evaluating ourselves, the Bible says we are to examine our *hearts*, making certain we are walking in faith and purity toward the Lord. (See 1 Corinthians 11:28 and 2 Corinthians 13:5.)

Second Timothy 1:6 exhorts us to stir up the gifts God has given us, and Jesus made it quite clear in the parable of the talents that we are to use all the abilities and resources God gives us to give glory to Him. (See Matthew 25:14-29.)

Whether we are examining our hearts or using the gifts and talents God gave us, our focus is always on the Lord. Our motivation is to please Him, draw closer to Him, and serve those He leads us to serve.

The irony of the Christian life is that when we give our lives to God and to others, we receive true joy and fulfillment. It is when we hold onto our lives and are consumed with our own selfish desires and interests that we are miserable and nonproductive.

Tonight take your mind off yourself and concentrate on your loving heavenly Father. Ask Him about His plan for your life. Focus on Him and where He wants to take you!

The Guiding Light

Your word is a lamp to my feet and a light for my path.
PSALM 119:105 NIV

D r. Alexander of Princeton once described a little glowworm which took a step so small it could hardly be measured. But as it moved across the fields at midnight, there was just enough light in its glow to light up the step ahead. As it moved forward, it always moved in the light.

At times we feel lost, like we are stumbling around in the dark. However, the Bible says, "The path of the righteous is like the first gleam of dawn, shining ever brighter till the full light of day." (Proverbs 4:18 NIV.) Just like the glowworm's path is lit as it continues to take each step, the light of the Word lights our every step.

An Englishman wrote in his diary of an "enlightening" experience he had one dark night: "When I was crossing the Irish Channel one starless night, I stood on the deck by the captain and asked him, 'How do you know Holyhead Harbor on so dark a night as this?'

"He said, 'You see those three lights? All of them must line up together as one, and when we see them so united, we know the exact position of the harbor's mouth.'"

Another scripture says, "In the mouth of two or three witnesses shall every word be established." (2 Corinthians 13:1.) The Word of God is one of those witnesses. The perfect peace of the Holy Spirit is another. And often, God will send a person or a circumstance to confirm we have heard from His Word and His Spirit. When those three "lights" line up, then you know where the "harbor" is.

The Word of God serves as a continuous light to evaluate our daily decisions, much like the light in the Cathedral of Florence. Built by Filippo Brunelleschi, the cathedral stands on marshy ground, so he left a small opening in the dome through which a shaft of light streams every June 21. The sunbeam squarely illuminates a brass plate set in the floor of the sanctuary. Should the ray fail to cover the plate completely, it would indicate the structure had shifted, and steps would need to be taken to deal with the emergency.

The Word of God is the light which tells you if you have shifted off the path God has set for you. Spend some time reading your Bible tonight and every night!

Stargazing

Then He brought him [Abraham] outside and said, "Look now toward heaven, and count the stars if you are able to number them." And He said to him, "So shall your descendants be."
GENESIS 15:5 NKJV

While visiting relatives in a rural area, a father decided to take his young daughter for an evening walk along a country road. The family lived in a large city, where walking at night was not the custom or considered safe. The father could hardly wait to see how his daughter would respond to a star-filled sky.

At first, his daughter was playful, exploring the flowers and insects along the edge of the dirt lane. As dusk turned into dark, however, she became a little fearful and clung to his hand tightly. She seemed grateful for the flashlight he had brought along. Suddenly, she looked toward the sky and exclaimed with surprise, "Daddy, somebody drew dots all over the sky!"

Her father smiled. His young daughter had never seen a night sky away from the city lights. He was glad the moon had not yet risen so the stars appeared even closer and more distinct. "Daddy," she continued in her enthusiasm, "if we connect them all will they make a picture?"

The night sky had taken on the quality of a dot-to-dot puzzle for his child! *What an interesting notion*, the father thought. "No," he replied to his daughter, "the dots are there for another purpose. Each one is a hope God has for your life. God loves you so much He has lots of hopes that your life will be filled with good things. In fact, there are more hopes than you or I can ever count!"

"I knew it!" the little girl said. "The dots *do* make a picture." And then she added more thoughtfully, "I always wondered what hope looked like."

When God showed Abraham the stars and asked Him to count them, he was giving him hope that the promise He had made to him, that he would have a son, was coming.

Whenever the sky is clear at night, do some stargazing! The stars are a picture of God's hope — for you, for your family, for the world. Stargazing is one of the best ways to get your earthy life back into perspective and realize in God's infinite universe, He has a specific plan for you, just as He did for Abraham.

———————————

The Father's Heart

I was eyes to the blind, and feet was I to the lame.
JOB 29:15

"When I was young I admired clever people. Now that I am old, I admire kind people," said Rabbi Abraham Heschel. From the Jewish perspective, an unkind person does not believe in God.

"How could anyone who believes in the God of the Bible treat his or her fellow human beings, all of whom are created in God's image, with less than compassion?" asks Rabbi Joseph Telushkin.

"Have we not all one Father? Did not one God create us? How then can we deal treacherously each man with his brother?" (Malachi 2:10)

The story is told that when Abba Tahnah the Pious was entering his city on the Sabbath eve with a bundle slung over his shoulder, he came upon a helpless man lying at a crossroads.

The man said to him, "Master, do an act of kindness for me. Carry me into the city."

146

Abba Tahnah replied, "If I abandon my bundle, how shall I and my household support ourselves? But if I abandon a man afflicted with boils, I will forfeit my life!"

He set down his bundle on the road and carried the afflicted man into the city. Then he returned for his bundle and reentered the city with the last rays of the sun. Everybody was astonished at seeing so pious a man carrying a heavy bundle as the Sabbath was beginning, something forbidden by Jewish law. They exclaimed, "Is this really Abba Tahnah the Pious?"

He too felt uneasy at heart and said to himself: "Is it possible that I have desecrated the Sabbath?" At that point, the Holy One caused the sun to continue to shine, thereby delaying the beginning of the Sabbath.[40]

Each kindly act we do toward men,
Each loving word by voice or pen,
Brings recompense in brotherhood,
And makes the Father understood.[41]

Pray tonight for opportunities to be kind tomorrow. While it may not be on your "to do" list for the day, and may delay a project, your kindnesses toward others count for eternity and show others the nature of your loving Father God.

Family Devotions

When you pray . . . pray to your Father who is in the secret place; and your Father who sees in secret will reward you openly.
MATTHEW 6:6 NKJV

Bedtime prayers are often limited to reciting a poem or saying a little memorized prayer. However, bedtime prayers can become family devotions if the entire family gathers at the bedside of the child who retires first.

Each member of the family says a heartfelt prayer that is spontaneous and unrehearsed. A verse or two of Scripture might be read prior to prayer. The point of such a devotional time is not that a child is obedient to say a prayer before sleep, but that the child's heart is knit to the heart of God and to the hearts of other family members.

Spontaneous, unrehearsed prayers invite a child to share their heart with the Lord. Having each family member pray allows the child to catch a glimpse of their souls and learn from their example how to relate to God, give praise, and make their requests known to a loving heavenly Father.

Albert Schweitzer once commented on the need for parents to provide an example in devotion:

"From the services in which I joined as a child I have taken with me into life a feeling for what is solemn, and a need for quiet self-recollection, without which I cannot realize the meaning of my life. I cannot, therefore, support the opinion of those who would not let children take part in grown-up people's services till they to some extent understand them. The important thing is not that they shall understand but that they shall feel something of what is serious and solemn. The fact that a child sees his elders full of devotion, and has to feel something of devotion himself, that is what gives the service its meaning for him."[42]

End your evening with family devotions. Even if you don't have children, it's an opportunity to spend time with your heavenly Father and sort out the chaos of the day. He'll help you put everything into perspective so you can sleep peacefully.

Strangers and Pilgrims

There will be no more death or mourning or crying or pain,
for the old order of things has passed away.
REVELATION 21:4 NIV

D ay in and day out, the details of everyday life can cause our attention to be focused on only the here and now. When change comes—the birth of a child, the first day of school, a new job, the death of a parent—it can be exciting, bittersweet, or even sad.

The first line of a hymn written by Albert E. Brumley gives us the perspective we should have toward the time we spend on this planet. "This world is not my home, I'm just a passing through."

In his book, *Strangers and Pilgrims*, W. R. Matthews describes how we should see ourselves. While he doesn't recommend a total detachment from the life that swirls around us, he advises:

"We should live in this world as if we did not wholly belong to it and . . . we should avoid that complete absorption in its vicissitudes into which the most eager spirits easily fall. It is wise to remind ourselves that even our most cherished ambitions and interests are passing; the soul will grow out of them or at least must leave them behind."

"To the pilgrim these passages should not be wholly sad," says Matthews. *"He may feel regret, but not desolation; they do not cause him to rebel. These phases of life are incidents of the journey, but it is the way that matters, not the accidents of the road. The time has come to move on? Then break up the camp with a good heart; it is only one more stage on the journey home!"*[43]

Home, of course, is heaven, one of the greatest anchors of our Christian life. When we remember our final destination is heaven, everything we are going through at the moment becomes clearer and more meaningful.

———————————————————

The Power of For-giveness

For if you forgive men when they sin against you, your heavenly Father will also forgive you.
MATTHEW 6:14 NIV

Unforgiveness is a destructive and insidious force, having more effect on the one who is unforgiving than on the unforgiven. A great example of this was an experience of one of the outstanding intellects of all history, Leonardo da Vinci.

Just before he commenced work on his depiction of the Last Supper, he had a violent quarrel with a fellow painter. Leonardo was so enraged and bitter, he determined to use the face of his enemy as the face of Judas, thus taking his revenge by handing the man down to succeeding generations in infamy and scorn.

The face of Judas was, therefore, one of the first that he finished, and everyone readily recognized it as the face of the painter with whom he had quarreled.

However, when he attempted to paint the face of Jesus Christ, Leonardo could make no progress. Something seemed to be baffling him—holding him back and frustrating his efforts. At length, he came to the conclusion that what was hindering and frustrating him was that he had painted his enemy into the face of Judas.

When he painted over the face of his enemy in the portrait of Judas, he commenced anew on the face of Jesus. This depiction became a success which has been acclaimed through the ages.

You cannot be painting the features of Jesus Christ into your own life, and at the same time be painting another face with the colors of enmity and hatred.

If you are harboring unforgiveness and bitterness, forgive your offender and put them and the situation in Gods hands. Ask Him to cleanse you of those negative feelings and to release you from their bondage. As you forgive, you will be forgiven and set free to live your life with inner peace.

The Small Stuff

Thou hast been faithful over a few things, I will make thee ruler over many things: enter thou into the joy of the lord.
MATTHEW 25:21

A man once said to his new bride, "Honey, I think the best way for our family to operate would be for you to take care of all the small stuff, and let me take care of all the big stuff." His young wife agreed, and so they lived their lives.

At the celebration of their fiftieth wedding anniversary, the couple was asked to share their "secret" to a happy marriage. The husband relayed the agreement they had made as newlyweds. His wife added with a smile, "And I discovered that if I took care of the small stuff, there never was any big stuff to handle!"

Clearing away the small stuff of life—the daily decisions, problem-solving, and nuisances that need to be resolved—can be regarded as a burden, or they can be viewed as paving the way to peace and productivity. It takes just as much effort to remove small stones from a path as it does to arrange them so they make a better path. It's all in your point of view.

This prayer by Mary Stuart reflects a desire to move beyond the small stuff into the truly meaningful:

Keep me, O Lord, from all pettiness. Let me be large in thought and word and deed.

Let me leave off self-seeking and have done with fault-finding.

Help me put away all pretense, that I may meet my neighbor face to face, without self-pity and without prejudice.

May I never be hasty in my judgments, but generous to all and in all things.

Make me grow calm, serene, and gentle . . .

Grant that I may realize that it is the trifling things of life that create differences, that in the higher things we are all one.

*And, O Lord, God, let me not forget to be kind!*44

When we handle the small things, we can move on to the greater things!

———————————————

Nothing to Fear

Let him who walks in the dark, who has no light, trust in the
name of the Lord and rely on his God.
ISAIAH 50:10 NIV

When we were kids, most of us enjoyed camping out in the back yard. Dad would help us put up the tent, and Mom would make sure we had plenty of provisions. With flashlights, pocketknives, and the faithful family dog for protection, we were ready to brave the elements—and anything else that might threaten our outpost.

What we didn't count on was the darkness. Those trees in the yard, so innocent by day, looked positively menacing at night. And we'd think, *What are those tiny lights that keep moving around and flickering off and on? What if we get attacked by a wild animal that just happened to wander into our neighborhood tonight? What if we yell for help and Mom and Dad don't hear us?* And then the idea hits us: *Maybe we could get Dad to camp out with us!*

Dad arrived with his sleeping bag and more provisions, without recriminations or condemnation. We fell asleep with no trouble at all. In our memories, the camp-out was a stunning success.

The world can be a scary place anytime there's darkness. Hard as we try to keep a stiff upper lip, sometimes we just have to say, "Father, help!"

The story is told of the Patons, missionaries who went to a forsaken island known for its cannibals and headhunters. In the early part of their ministry, Paton and his wife slept on the beach each night. The natives watched them from nearby bushes, but never came near.

Thirty fruitful years of ministry later, one of their native converts asked Paton, "Those nights you and your wife slept on the beach . . . what was that army we saw surrounding the two of you?" Paton, of course, had no army, but he knew beyond a doubt who the "soldiers" were, and that God had sent them.[45]

The God who watches over "your going out and your coming in" (Psalm 121:8 NKJV) can be counted on to protect you from the darkness of evil. Trust in His power, His love, and His name to keep you through the night, whatever darkness you may face.

Ultimate Worth

You are Christ's, and Christ is God's.
1 *CORINTHIANS 3:23 NKJV*

―――――――――――――――

"Going . . . going . . . gone!" The bidding was over and the auctioneer's gavel fell. The winning bid for a rocking chair that had been valued between $3,000 and $5,000 was $453,500.

This had been the case through the duration of the auction. A used automobile valued between $18,000 and $22,000 was sold for $79,500. A set of green tumblers valued at $500 sold for $38,000. A necklace valued at $500 to $700 went for $211,500. For four days articles of common, ordinary value were sold for wildly inflated prices. Why? The items auctioned were from the estate of Jacqueline Kennedy Onassis.

How do we assess value? How do we determine what is valuable to us?

As in the sale of the items of the Kennedy estate, some things are valuable solely because of the one to whom they belong. Paul wrote to the Corinthians, "You were bought at a price" (1 Corinthians 6:20 NKJV).

Peter wrote, "You were not redeemed with corruptible things, like silver or gold . . . but with the precious blood of Christ" (1 Peter 1:18-19 NKJV). The price Paul and Peter are talking about was the price for our sin, paid by Jesus Christ in His death on the cross.

We may inflate a person's worth because of their financial status, their influence, or their potential to benefit us; or we may say a person has no value because they have few assets or cannot help us. But the Scriptures tell us that when we were still sinners Jesus Christ died for us. (See Romans 5:8.) When we had no value and were even opposed to God, He paid the price to redeem our lives.

Every individual on the face of the earth is someone for whom Jesus died. Because of the great price of redemption, every single person, regardless of their financial worth, is of great importance.

Whenever you feel depressed and worthless, meditate on this: Your value is determined by God. He loved and valued you so much, He sent His Son to die so you could become His child. Never doubt your importance and worth!

God Is Awake

He will not let your foot slip – he who watches over you will not slumber; indeed, he who watches over Israel will neither slumber nor sleep.
PSALM 121:3-4 NIV

Anna was alone in her new home for the first time since moving into the city. Jake's new job meant they would someday be able to buy a home of their own in a safer part of town. But for now, they could only afford a rental house in a section where drug deals and streetwalkers were a daily sight.

Jake left on a business trip early one day, admonishing her as he left to be sure all the windows and doors were secure before she and Daisy went to bed that night. "We'll be okay" she assured him. "God has always taken care of us, and He knows we need His protection and peace more than ever."

The memory of her words made her smile a bit in retrospect. She wasn't feeling very peaceful when evening actually arrived. As she checked the last door lock, she thought she heard people yelling somewhere down the street, which made her even more tense.

When she reached Daisy's room, she found her daughter sitting in a little ball in the middle of her bed. Her wide eyes told Anna that she had heard the yelling, too.

"Mom, do we have to turn out the lights tonight?" Daisy pleaded. Anna had not left the lights on for Daisy since she was four. The bright country moon had provided enough light to wean her away from the night light. But Gods lamp, as they had called it, was nowhere to be seen in this smoggy city atmosphere.

"Honey, do you really need it?" Anna asked.

"Yes! I can't see God's lamp tonight. He must have already gone to bed."

"Sweetie, God never sleeps. Even when you can't see His lamp He's up there watching over you."

"Well," Daisy replied, "as long as God is awake, there is no sense in both of us staying awake!"

As you turn off the lights and climb into bed tonight, your fears may not be the same as Daisy's, but the same truth can comfort you. God is awake! He's always watching over you, ready to protect you from harm.

Night Sounds

*I will bless the Lord who counsels me; he gives me wisdom in
the night. He tells me what to do.*
P S A L M   1 6 : 7   T L B

T he night seems to have different sounds and
rhythms than the day. It isn't necessarily
that the specific sounds of the night are
louder or exclusively belonging to the night, although
some are. Rather, it is at night that we seem to hear certain sounds more clearly. It is at night that we are likely
to notice:

The ticking of a clock.
The creak of a stair.
The chirp of a cricket.
The barking of a dog.
The scrape of a twig against the window.
The clatter of a loose shutter.

The deep call of a foghorn.
The wind in the trees.

The croaking of a frog.
The opening of a door.
The strains of music down the hall.
The whimper of a child.
The whispers of a spouse.

It is also at night that we are more prone to listen with our spiritual ears. Frederick Buechner has suggested, "Listen to your life. See it for the fathomless mystery that it is. In the boredom and pain of it no less than in the excitement and gladness: touch, taste, smell your way to the holy and hidden heart of it because in the last analysis all moments are key moments, and life itself is grace."[46]

Listen to the moment.
Listen to your thoughts and feelings.
Listen to your impulses and desires.
Listen to your longings and fears.
Listen to the beat of your own heart.
Listen to God's still small voice in the innermost recesses
of your being.

Night is for listening. Listen—and learn—with your spiritual ears, as well as your natural ears.

_____

Out of Sight

*So then, just as you received Christ Jesus as Lord, continue
to live in him, rooted and built up in him, strengthened in
the faith as you were taught and overflowing with thankfulness.*
COLOSSIANS 2:6-7 NIV

A tree is nothing without its roots, and for the most part they do their job under-ground. Young roots absorb water and minerals from the soil. Older roots take these materials and send them into the stem.

In order to keep the tree going during dormant pe-riods, the roots store food, similar to the way a bear builds bulk to get him through hibernation. Food stored in the tree's roots provides energy and food needed when the weather changes and it's time for new growth.

Trees never stop growing. As long as they live, some type of growth is taking place. New roots are forming, new branches are appearing, or old bark is being sloughed off so that new bark can take its place.

Without the roots to lend mechanical support, act as anchors, and store food, a tree would fall.

The God Who cares enough about trees to set up an intricate feeding system for them gives each of us the food, water, and air we require to survive. He gives us family and friends, opportunities, and provision to accomplish His plan for our lives. We can't "see" God with our physical eyes, but like the finely developed web of roots beneath the ground, we know He's there, working on our behalf. That is His nature as Jehovah Jireh—the God who provides.

Have you ever been hungry? Jesus is the bread of life; He promises that whoever comes to Him will never go hungry. (See John 6:35.)

Have you ever been thirsty? As Jesus told the Samaritan woman at the well, "Whoever drinks the water I give him will never thirst" (John 4:14 NIV).

Do you ever find yourself gasping for breath? Job knew who to thank for the air we all breathe? "In his hand is the life of every creature and the breath of all mankind" (Job 12:10 NIV).

Stay rooted in the Lord and watch Him provide for your every need!

Praying Grandmoth-ers

The eyes of the Lord run to and fro throughout the whole earth, to shew himself strong in the behalf of them whose heart is perfect toward him.
2 CHRONICLES 16:9

For fifty years Sister Agnes and Mrs. Baker had prayed for their nation of Latvia to be freed from Soviet oppression. Most of all, they prayed for the freedom to worship in their Methodist Church in Leipaja. When the atheistic Soviet regime came to power, the enemy invaders took over their church building and turned the sanctuary into a sports hall.

Their prayers were answered in 1991, when the oppression came to an end. The Soviets left and the tiny nation was free. But it needed to be rebuilt, and Sister Agnes and Mrs. Baker were determined to help.

First the two women, now past 80, talked to a local minister. They said if he would agree to be their pastor, they would be his first members. A church was reborn!

Next they had to regain ownership of the building. That done, they began getting the church ready for worship services. One of the church members undertook painting the 25-foot-high walls. For weeks she mounted scaffolding and painted the walls and ceiling. The tall Palladian windows were cleaned to a bright, gleaming shine, and the wood floor was restored to a rich luster.

Because of careful record keeping by church members, the original church pews were found in storage out in the country. They were returned and put in place for worshipers. Sister Agnes had kept the church pump organ safe in her own home, so she returned it to the sanctuary. When she wasn't directing the choir, she played it with great enthusiasm.

God had been faithful! Lenin had predicted Christianity would die out within a generation. After the grandmothers died, he said, there would be no more Christians left. But he didn't know Sister Agnes and Mrs. Baker and the God they loved!

God wants to show Himself strong on your behalf, just as He did for Mrs. Baker and Sister Agnes. Jesus said, "I will build my church; and the gates of hell will not prevail against it" (Matthew 16:18).

You are part of His church and He will not let evil triumph over you! No matter what you are facing tonight, have faith that He will bring you through.

Providence

But I have raised you up for this very purpose, that I might show you my power and that my name might be proclaimed in all the earth.

EXODUS 9:16 NIV

February 26, 1844, is one of the most infamous dates in the history of the United States Navy. The most powerful warship of that time, the *Princeton*, was taking the President of the United States, the Secretaries of State and Navy, members of Congress, and other government officials down the Potomac.

For the entertainment of the guests, the great gun on the *Princeton*, the Peacemaker, was fired. At the second discharge, the gun burst apart, killing the Secretary of the Navy and a number of others.

Just before the gun was fired, Senator Thomas Benton of Missouri was standing near it. A friend laid his hand on his shoulder. Benton turned away to speak with him, and much to Bentons annoyance, Secretary of the Navy Gilmore elbowed his way into his place. At precisely that moment the gun was fired and Gilmore was killed.

That singular moment of providence had a great impression upon Benton. He was a man of anger and feuding, and had recently had a fierce quarrel with Daniel Webster. But after his narrow escape from death on the *Princeton*, Benton sought reconciliation with Webster.

He said to him, "It seemed to me, Mr. Webster, as if that touch on my shoulder was the hand of the Almighty stretched down there drawing me away from what otherwise would have been instantaneous death. That one circumstance has changed the whole current of my thought and life. I feel that I am a different man; and I want in the first place to be at peace with all those with whom I have been so sharply at variance."

Few of us ever know the many times we are spared from death, but in reality each day we live is a gift from God. Enjoy each day heartily and use the time wisely. And no matter how long you live, never waste a day in anger or unforgiveness. Live each day in peace with God and your fellow man.

Faithfulness

"The Lord is my portion," says my soul, "therefore I hope in Him!"

LAMENTATIONS 3:24 NKJV

Many people seem to believe God has called them to live successful lives. In fact, He calls each one of us to live *faithful* lives—lives of obedience, devotion, worship, and service.

With each day there often remains a residue of things left undone, unsaid, unachieved, or unconquered. Each day has its own measure of failure, its own degree of trouble (Matthew 6:34), and its own lingering doubts.

As you conduct a full review of your day—the bad as well as the good—it may be helpful to recall these words of Annie Johnson Flint:

"WHAT GOD HATH PROMISED?"

God hath not promised

Skies always blue,
Flower-strewn pathways
All our lives through;
God hath not promised
Sun without rain,
Joy without sorrow,
Peace without pain.

But God hath promised
Strength for the day,
Rest for the labor,
Light for the way,
Grace for the trials,
Help from above,
Unfailing sympathy,
Undying love.[47]

You may not have been as successful today as *you* would have liked, but every day you are faithful to the Lord is a success for *Him*. Remember the things He has promised and that regardless of your performance today, as you give your whole heart to Him, He makes up the difference.

———————————

Rituals

A heart at peace gives life to the body.
PROVERBS 14:30 NIV

————————————————

The word "ritual" is derived from the word, "rite," which means "a ceremonial or formal, solemn act, observance, or procedure in accordance with prescribed rule or custom."[48] A ritual refers to a system of rites—in other words, doing the same thing in the same way, every time. Rituals are common customs unique to an era or group of people.

The word rite originally had a religious connotation. The best-known rites of the church, in the past as well as the present, have been baptism, communion, joining the church, marriage, and burial. These rites give a comforting continuity when the meanings remain alive and cherished.

For example, when a new convert and the congregation understand that water baptism is a outward statement of what has already taken place inwardly— the "old man" has died with Jesus Christ (going under the water) and is raised with Jesus Christ (coming out of the water) — the baptismal service becomes a powerful time of worship.

On a more mundane level, in present day society a ritual can be anything performed on a regular basis. It can now refer to something as simple as brushing our teeth. Whether we realize it or not, we all have rituals. The things we do to prepare for work in the morning and the things we do when we get home each night are rituals that give order, meaning, and security to our lives.

Just like religious rituals, our daily rituals can bring us peace and comfort or leave us frustrated and lifeless. Our daily routine should include rituals which balance and enhance our lives spiritually, mentally, emotionally, socially, professionally, and physically.

A devotional time before bed touches every area. Praying purifies the heart, reading the Word of God renews the mind, receiving more of the heavenly Fathers unconditional love evokes feelings of serenity, communing with the Lord gives us a sense of belonging and guides us in our work — and all these things put the body in a relaxed, peaceful state.

In His Eyes

The eyes of the Lord are upon the righteous.
P S A L M   3 4 : 1 5

Sandra Palmer Carr describes a touching moment with one of her sons in *The Upper Room*. When her younger son Boyd was four years old, she was rocking him in a high-backed wooden rocking chair, as was her habit. But this time he was facing her, straddling her lap with his knees bent.

Suddenly, he sat up straight, lifted his head and stared intensely into her eyes. He became very still, and Sandra stopped rocking. He cupped her face in his little hands and said in a near-whisper, "Mommy, I'm in your eyes."

They stayed that way for several long moments, staring into one another's eyes. The rocking stopped and the room grew quiet. Then Sandra whispered back, "And I'm in yours." Boyd leaned his head against her contentedly, and they resumed their rocking.

In the days that followed, Boyd would often check to see if his discovery still held true. "Am I still in your eyes. Mommy?" he would ask, reaching up to her. She would pull him close to her so he could look in her eyes and see for himself — he was still there![49]

How can we be assured we are always in Gods eyes? The Bible has many, many verses to indicate He is continuously thinking of us, attending to us, and doing all He can to bless us. Certainly, Jesus' death and resurrection are a constant reminder of how dear and precious we are to Him.

One of the best times to stop and see yourself in Gods eyes is just before falling asleep. Your heavenly Father desires to rock you to sleep in His love, letting you stop now and then to call to mind a verse of Scripture that tells you how much you mean to Him.

You should never doubt you are the focus of God's tender care and attention. You can have a grateful and confident heart knowing you are always in his eyes.

God's Cloud of Protection

For this God is our God for ever and ever; He will be our guide even to the end.
PSALM 48:14 NIV

———————————————

During World War II, one of our mighty bombers took off from the island of Guam with its deadly cargo. Its target was Kokura, Japan. The sleek B-29 circled above the cloud that covered Kokura for half an hour, then three-quarters of an hour, then 55 minutes.

Finally, their gas supply reached the danger point and they were ordered to fly to a secondary target. It seemed a shame to be right over the primary target and have to pass it up, but there was no choice.

With one more look back, the crew headed for the secondary target, where the sky proved clear. "Bombs away!"—and the B-29 headed for home.

Weeks later, an officer received information from military intelligence that sent a chill through his heart.

Thousands of Allied prisoners of war, the biggest concentration of Americans in enemy hands, had been moved to Kokura a week before the suspended bombing!

"Thank God," breathed the officer. "Thank God for that cloud."

The city which was hidden from the bomber was the site of a massive prison camp, and a simple cloud saved the lives of thousands of Americans. The secondary target that day was Nagasaki. The bomb intended for Kokura was the world's second atomic bomb!

You must make choices every moment of the day. Often those choices affect the lives of others, and at times these decisions are heart wrenching. In these moments, it is important to remember that you can trust God for His guidance, His wisdom, and His divine protection. Even when we can't see beyond the circumstances and may be afraid to go on, God can see and will lead you in the right path.

After the Uproar

And after the uproar was ceased, Paul called unto him the
disciples, and embraced them.
ACTS 20:1

For a small child, the most comforting place in the world is in the secure arms of his mother or father. It's not really very different for grown-ups. The embrace of caring arms is a wonderful place to be. Even a brief hug from a casual friend can lift one's spirits.

At the end of a busy or frustrating day, "after the uproar has ceased," grown-ups may long for a pair of loving parental arms to assure them everything's going to be all right — to hear a voice that says soothingly, "I'm here, and I'll take care of you."

Take this little poem as a "hug" this evening from One Who loves you without measure, and Who watches over your every move with tenderness and compassion:

When the birds begin to worry

And the lilies toil and spin,
And God's creatures all are anxious,
Then I also may begin.

For my Father sets their table,
Decks them out in garments fine,
And if He supplies their living,
Will He not provide for mine?

Just as noisy, common sparrows
Can be found most anywhere —
Unto some just worthless creatures,
If they perish who would care?

Yet our Heavenly Father numbers
Every creature great and small,
Caring even for the sparrows,
Marking when to earth they fall.

If His children's hairs are numbered,
Why should we be filled with fear?
He has promised all that's needful,
And in trouble to be near.

UNKNOWN

The Art of Peace

You will keep in perfect peace him whose mind is steadfast.
ISAIAH 26:3 NIV

In the midst of violence, terror, or war, is it possible to find an island of peace? Where does one go to experience tranquillity?

The one place no one would expect to find peace is in the court of the Yugoslav War Crimes Tribunal, convened in The Hague. Certainly the president of that court needed some way to escape from the horrible stories that were crossing his desk regarding Bosnia.

How did Antonio Cassese supplant the gruesome images of man's inhumanity? By paying a visit to the Mauritshuis Museum in the center of town and filling his head with the beautiful images of paintings by Johannes Vermeer.

What is it about Vermeer that inspired Cassese? He says it was the peacefulness and serenity of the works.

Peace and serenity? That's hardly the world that Vermeer knew! He lived in Europe during a period of tumult and conflict. England and the United Provinces of the Netherlands, Vermeer's homeland, were at war three times during his 42 years. Vermeer also had many children, numerous debts, and suffered a humiliating bankruptcy. How could his paintings embody peace? The following story gives us a clue.

During a political crisis some years back, a young man and several of his compatriots had allowed themselves to become overwrought about the situation in their homeland. An historian from England spoke with the group, and reminded them of the story of Jesus calming the waters. (See Matthew 8:23-27.) "It seems to me," this historian said, "that in the midst of a storm, you shouldn't let the tumult enter you. The thing to do is get in touch with the peace that resides inside of you and let it out."

Vermeer tapped into a peace he harbored inside himself and shared it with others through his paintings. Cassese was receiving that same peace from his paintings many years later.[50]

The peace inside of you has a powerful name—Jesus. Keep your mind on Him tonight, and watch the storms of your life fade to the background.

Restoration

But those who hope in the Lord will renew their strength.
They will soar on wings like eagles; they will run and not
grow weary, thy will walk and not be faint.
ISAIAH 40:31 NIV

In a remote Swiss village stood a beautiful church. It was known as the Mountain Valley Cathedral. The church was not only beautiful to look at, with its high pillars and magnificent stained glass windows, but it had the most incredible pipe organ in the entire region. People would come from miles away—even from far-off lands—to hear the lovely tones of this organ.

One day a problem arose. The columns were still there, the windows still dazzled with the sunlight, but an eerie silence enveloped the valley. The area no longer echoed with the glorious fine-tuned music of the pipe organ.

Musicians and experts from around the world tried to repair the instrument. Every time a new person would try to fix it the villagers were subjected to sounds of disharmony, awful noises that seemed to pollute the air.

One day an old man appeared at the church door. He spoke with the sexton, and after a time the sexton reluctantly agreed to let the old man try his hand at repairing the organ. For two days the old man worked in almost total silence. The sexton was getting a bit nervous.

Then on the third day, at precisely high noon, the valley once again was filled with glorious music. Farmers dropped their plows, merchants closed their stores, everyone in town stopped what they were doing and headed for the Cathedral. Even the bushes and trees of the mountain tops seemed to respond as the glorious music echoed from ridge to ridge.

After the old man finished playing, a brave soul asked him how he could have restored the magnificent instrument when the world's experts could not. The old man merely said, "It was I who built this organ fifty years ago. I created it—and now I have restored it."

God created you, and He knows exactly what you need to live your life to the fullest. As your Creator, He can restore you at the end of a draining day—so you can play beautiful music tomorrow!

Benediction

And the very God of peace sanctify you wholly; and I pray God your whole spirit and soul and body be preserved blameless unto the coming of our Lord Jesus Christ.
1 THESSALONIANS 5:23

A benediction is the pronouncing of a divine blessing. It is usually associated with the final words of a worship service, given by a spiritual leader, but you can give yourself a benediction right where you are, this very night!

The only requirement for a benediction is this: that no sin or unforgiveness stands between you and the Lord Jesus Christ. If you question the purity of your heart, tonight is a good time to ask the Lord to cleanse you and renew a right spirit within you.

Then face yourself in a mirror before you turn off the lights for the night and pronounce a benediction upon yourself. Speak it with faith and boldness, in full confidence that the Lord desires this blessing to take root in you and bear good fruit. If you have a family, you may want to pronounce a blessing on them, or each member individually.

By doing so you can end each day with a keen awareness of God's blessing and His claim on your life.

The benediction inscribed at Gloucester Cathedral is one you may want to use:

Go on your way in peace.
Be of good courage.
Holdfast that which is good.
Render to no man evil for evil.
Strengthen the fainthearted.
Support the weak.
Help and cheer the sick.
Honor all men.
Love and serve the Lord.
May the blessing of God be upon you
And remain with you forever.

So be it. And have a blessed good night!

20/20 Vision

Let your light shine before men, that they may see your good
deeds and praise your Father in heaven.
MATTHEW 5:16 NIV

Marine biologists are learning a great deal about the ocean floor these days, thanks to the specially designed one-person submarine. Able to stay submerged for up to eight hours at a time and capable of going as deep as one kilometer, these subs give new meaning to "ocean view"—compliments of a transparent passenger housing made of acrylic. Subs are outfitted with lights, electric thrusters, hydraulic manipulator arms, and scientific, navigational, and life-support equipment.

Despite all the high-tech gadgets, however, this fact remains: It's dark down there! Sunlight only travels so far. After a certain point, some other light source is needed if you're going to observe the wonders of the deep.

The same is true for the deep-sea creatures, many of which emit a form of natural illumination known as bioluminescence. For some, the built-in lighting is used as a defense system. Enemies are sprayed with glowing tissue that turns the hunter into the hunted.

For others, the light provides camouflage. What little sunlight pierces the darkness above them works with the light coming from the creatures' undersides and erases any shadows that might give away their position.[51]

Few of us will ever sink to the level of these creatures, but we understand how they must feel about light. When we're driving on a poorly-lit road late at night, we rely on our car's headlights to keep us from driving off the pavement. We protect our house from break-ins by putting floodlights in the yard.

To live in this dark and confusing world, the Lord has put into us His own light, the Holy Spirit. He reveals what is true and good, as well as where we should and should not go. He is our conscience and our guide.

Looking back over your day, can you pinpoint times when the Holy Spirit was giving you direction or indicating what was wrong or right?

On the Wings of Prayer

May my prayer be set before you like incense; may the lifting up of my hands be like the evening sacrifice.
PSALM 141:2 NIV

The psalmist paints a beautiful word picture in this verse. Incense, so precious to the ancient world, covered the stench of everyday life with beauty. Incense also speaks of the spirit and essence of a person being "exhaled" in complete surrender to the Lord.

Hands raised to the Lord are hands at rest, for such hands cannot be toiling or creating mischief. Raised hands also speak of complete surrender to and reliance upon the Lord. The total image is one of spiritual beauty—childlike faith reaching to touch the heart and receive the embrace of a loving heavenly Father.

This atmosphere for evening prayer is captured well in a poem by R. E. Neighbour:

I breathed a heartfelt evening prayer
To God on high, and lingered there,
To see if God did truly care
In heaven above.
Down from the heights, my answer came
A quiet peace passed through my frame,
I felt His presence, praise His Name
For God is love.

I sang a joyful, evening song,
It swept the stars, its way along,
And up amid that heavenly throng,
Reached God on high:
Then, back into my spirit came,
God's presence, as a bush aflame,
I bowed again and praised His Name,
For God was nigh.

How wonderful to have the right,
Up past the stars to take our flight,
Into God's holy, sacred light,
Beyond the blue;
There to have access by His grace,
Into the presence of His face,
And then, to earth, our way retrace,
With hope anew.[52]

Finishing Well

As he had begun, so he would also complete this grace in you.
2 CORINTHIANS 8:6 NKJV

———————————

Putting the finish on a piece of furniture is the final step in its construction. The bulk of the work that gives the chest, table, or chair its *function* happens much earlier in the process. But it is the finish—the staining and varnishing—that very often gives a piece of furniture its *beauty*. The finish brings out the grain and luster of the wood, the smoothness of the craftsmanship, and the shine that speaks of completion.

The cross on which Jesus was crucified marked the end of His earthly life. As He exhaled His last breath He declared, "It is finished." This was a triumphant statement that marked the completion of His earthly mission to satisfy and fulfill God's law for all mankind. The cross became the beacon that shines brightly into sinful hearts and says, "You can be free." It also became the prelude for a "new beginning," at His resurrection—offering new life for all.

We are each called to end our lives well, but our finish is not simply at our death. It is also in our bringing closure to each day in such a way that we allow for our resurrection the following morning. It is saying with thankfulness and humility, "I've done what the Lord put before me to do today, to the best of my ability. And now, I give my all to Him anew so that He might recreate me and use me again tomorrow."

Ralph Waldo Emerson offered this advice: "Finish every day and be done with it. You have done what you could. Some blunders and absurdities no doubt crept in; forget them as soon as you can. Tomorrow is a new day; begin it well and serenely and with too high a spirit to be cumbered with your old nonsense. This day is all that is good and fair. It is too dear, with its hopes and invitations, to waste a moment on yesterday's."

Amen! The God who began a good work in you, will finish it day by day, and ultimately bring it to completion (see Philippians 1:6).

———————————————

Sweet Sleep

In vain you rise early and stay up late, toiling for food to eat
— for he grants sleep to those he loves.
P S A L M   1 2 7 : 2

"Take two aspirin and call me in the morning." What is a doctor really saying when he gives you that instruction? In a way he's saying, "Get a good night's sleep and see if you don't feel better in the morning." It's amazing how well that works! Very often, we do feel better the next morning.

Scientific research supports that theory. In one study, laboratory rats died of fatal blood infections after being deprived of sleep for long periods of time — possibly because their immune systems failed.

Have you ever spent a few nights in a hospital, specifically in the intensive care unit? A patient's common complaint might be, "How am I supposed to get well when they keep waking me up every few hours?" Good point.

The frequent wake-ups, the noise, and the lights are believed to contribute to a slower rate of recovery. In fact, some patients wind up with ICU syndrome: hallucinations, disorientation, and depression that strike after about three days in the unit. The cause? Probably lack of sleep.

Being stubborn human beings, most of us ignore the bed-rest portion of a doctor's prescription when we have a less serious ailment, such as a cold or the flu. As long as we have to stay home, why not get something done? After all, we aren't dying.

Too often, however, a minor illness becomes something major, and then we have to take to our beds. How much time and trouble we could have saved if we had followed our doctor's orders to begin with? How much healthier would we be if we worked with our immune systems instead of against them?[53]

Writer Aldous Huxley has said, "That we are not much sicker and much madder than we are is due exclusively to that most blessed and blessing of all natural graces, sleep."

Sleep. Enjoy every minute of it!

Fruit Production

No branch can bear fruit by itself; it must remain in the
vine. Neither can you bear fruit unless you remain in me.
JOHN 15:4 NIV

Y ou may be familiar with the fruit of the
Spirit: love, joy, peace, patience, kindness,
goodness, faithfulness, gentleness, and self-
control. (See Galatians 5:22-23). How do we produce
this fruit? For one thing, it is impossible to manufac-
ture it. It cannot be store-bought or mass-produced. A
person can try to put on a mask of "joy" or a facade of
"gentleness," but sooner or later the superficial veneer
will crack.

"Fake fruit," writes Joni Eareckson Tada, "comes
from self-effort." She said, "It's like growing grapes the
wrong way around. First you find a cluster of white
Concords and fasten them to the branches of a vine.
From there, you tie roots to the trunk and dig a hole,
setting the entire thing into the ground. There you have
it, manufactured fruit (and incidentally, fruit that will
rot quickly). What you have done is put first the fruit;

second, the branches; third, the root; and fourth, the soil."

This is exactly backwards from the way God produces fruit. The fruit He produces is fruit that lasts for all eternity.

Tada describes God's way of producing fruit: "First He plants the seed of His Word in the soil of our heart. The Spirit quickens us and causes the Word to take root in our soul. Next, as we grow in the Lord, the vine and branches mature until sweet and satisfying fruit clusters in abundance.

"Genuine fruit," she concludes, "comes from abiding in the Vine."[54]

Our patience wears thin when we don't see the fruit we want to see in our lives. But have you ever noticed, you never heard an apple tree groaning as the apples formed on its branches? As long as the tree gets enough sunshine and water, fruit is formed naturally.

Our job is not to bear fruit—our job is to abide in the Vine and submit to the Vinedresser. When we do that, the Spirit (sunshine) and Word of God (water) are reigning in our hearts and minds. We are being transformed into the image of Jesus Christ, and the fruit grows and develops as a result.

Smooth Sailing

God is light and in Him is no darkness at all.
1 JOHN 1:5 NKJV

Dwight L. Moody used to tell this story about darkness and light.

"There was a terrible storm one night on Lake Erie. The captain of a ship could see the light from a lighthouse, but, not seeing the lower lights of the harbor, he questioned his pilot about their location.

"'Yes, sir, this is Cleveland,' the pilot said. The lower lights have gone out, sir.'

"'Will we make it into the harbor?'

"'If we don't, we're lost, sir,' the pilot replied.

"The pilot did his best, but it wasn't enough. Without the lower lights to guide them in, the ship crashed on the rocks."

Light is crucial if we want to get to our destination without mishap or error, especially if we want to reach the height of all we believe to be our destiny. Sometimes we might be tempted to try and fight our way through the darkness to prove we're smart enough or tough enough to sail through anything on our own. At other moments, courage fails us and fear blinds us to the light that's right in front of us.

Instead of trying to go on alone, or closing our eyes, we must realize there's a Light available to all of us. One guaranteed to guide us through darkness, fog, storms, and anything else that might hinder our progress.

Jesus Christ said, "I am the light of the world. Whoever follows me will never walk in darkness, but will have the light of life" (John 8:12).

As you climb into bed and turn out the lights tonight, remind yourself that the Light within you never dims or goes out. Keep your eyes focused on Jesus, and you will have a safe trip into the harbor!

———————————————

Sunset

May the God of hope fill you with all joy and peace in believing.
R O M A N S   1 5 : 1 3   N A S B

F. W. Boreham tells the story in *Boulevards of Paradise* of an elderly man taking a walk with his granddaughter. They met a man who poured out to them a long story of the difficulties of his life. He then apologized, explaining that he was suffering from a slight sunstroke.

As the grandfather and his little granddaughter departed, the little girl exclaimed, "Grandpa, I do hope that you will never suffer from a sunset!"

John Lloyd Ogilvie makes an important observation from this tender scene. He writes, "The point is all too clear. We suffer from a sunset before the day is ended. This is not only true for people who give up the adventure of growing spiritually and intellectually in the 'sunset' years of their lives, but also for Christians of every age who stop adventuring with Christ . . . We can be spiritually geriatric in our twenties or forties!"[55]

Wise sages have given us this perspective on aging:

- "You are as young as your faith, as old as your doubt; as young as your self-confidence, as old as your fear; as young as your hope, as old as your despair."
- "In the central place of every heart there is a recording chamber. So long as it receives messages of beauty, hope, cheer, and courage—so long are you young."
- "When your heart is covered with the snows of pessimism and the ice of cynicism, then and only then are you grown old."[56]

We should think of the glorious colors and magnificence of the sunsets we have seen as we approach the "sunset" times of our lives—the end of a day, a project, a journey, or some other significant season of life.

Sunset is a time of reflection. In nature, a sunset brings a brilliant and satisfying splendor to our souls *every day*. Spiritually, sunset is the time we pause to meditate on God's awesome creation, both around us and inside of us *every day*.

Take time every evening you can to view with wonder the spectacular event we know as a sunset. This is your heavenly Father's gift to you, filling you with gratitude for a day well spent with Him, the sweet sleep He will now give to you, and the hope and expectancy of spending tomorrow with Him.

References

Unless otherwise indicated, all Scripture quotations are taken from the *King James Version* of the Bible.

Scripture quotations marked NIV are taken from the *Holy Bible, New International Version*® Niv®. Copyright © 1973, 1978, 1984 by International Bible Society. Used by permission of Zondervan Publishing House. All rights reserved.

Scripture quotations marked NKJV are taken from *The New King James Version* of the Bible. Copyright © 1979, 1980, 1982, 1994 by Thomas Nelson, Inc., Publishers. Used by permission.

Scripture quotations marked AMP are taken from *The Amplified Bible, Old Testament.* Copyright © 1965 by Zondervan Publishing House, Grand Rapids, Michigan. *New Testament* copyright © 1958 by The Lockman Foundation, La Habra, California. Used by permission.

Scripture quotations marked RSV are taken from *The Revised Standard Version Bible*, copyright © 1952 by the Division of Christian Education of the Churches of Christ in the United States of America and is used by permission.

Scripture quotations marked NASB are taken from the *New American Standard Bible*. Copyright © 1960,

Endnotes

1. *Unto the Hills: A Devotional Treasury*, Billy Graham (Waco, TX: Word Books, 1986), p. 130.

2. *Spiritual Fitness*, Doris Donnelly (NY: HarperSanFrancisco, A Division of HarperCollins, 1993) p. 155-156, 165-66.

3. *The Christian's Secret of a Happy Life*, Hannah Whitall Smith, p. 38-40.

4. *Give Your Life a Lift*, Herman W Gockel (St. Louis: Concordia Publishing House, 1968), p. 114.

5. *Unto the Hills: A Devotional Treasury*, Billy Graham, (Waco, TX: Word Books, 1986), p. 158.

6. *The Last Word*, Jamie Buckingham (Plainfield, NJ: Logos International, 1978), p. 169-170.

7. *Unto the Hills: A Devotional Treasury*, Billy Graham (Waco, TX: Word Books, 1986), p. 223.

8. *Decision*, March 1996, p. 33.

9. "Who Switched the Price Tags?" Tony Campolo, *The Inspirational Study Bible*, Max Lucado, ed., (Dallas: Word Publishing, 1995) p. 402.

10. *Illustrations Unlimited*, James W. Hewett, ed. (Wheaton: Tyndale House, 1988) p. 25-26.

11. *A Moment a Day*, Mary Beckwith and Kathi Mills, ed., (Ventura, CA: Regal Books, 1988), p. 25.

12. *Ibid*, p. 37.

13. *101 More Hymn Stories*, Kenneth W Osbeck (Grand Rapids, MI: Kregel Publications, 1985), p. 24-26.

14. "Won by One," Ron Rand, *The Inspirational Study Bible*, Max Lucado, ed. (Dallas: Word, 1995), pp. 604- 605.

15. *A Moment a Day*, Mary Beckwith and Kathi Mills, ed. (Ventura, CA: Regal Books, 1988), p. 174.

16. *Newsweek*, November 27, 1995, p. 62-63.

17. *A Moment a Day*, Mary Beckwith and Kathi Mills, ed. (Ventura, CA: Regal Books, 1988), p. 184.

18. *Knight's Master Book of 4,000 Illustrations*, Walter B. Knight, (Grand Rapids, MI: Eerdmans Publishing Co., 1956), p. 448.

19. *Ibid*.

20. *A Moment a Day*, Mary Beckwith and Kathi Mills, ed. (Ventura, CA: Regal Books, 1988), p. 247.

21. *The Joy of Working*, Denis Waitley and Reni L. Witt (NY: Dodd, Mead & Company, 1985), p. 213-214.

22. *Songs of My Soul: Devotional Thoughts from the Writings of W. Phillip Keller*, Al Bryant, ed. (Dallas: Word, 1989), p. 77.

23. *You Don't Have to Be Blind to See*, Jim Stovall (Nashville, TN: Thomas Nelson Publishers, 1996), p. 90.

24. *101 More Hymn Stories*, Kenneth W Osbeck (Grand Rapids, Ml: Kregel Publications, 1985), p. 274-277.

25. *Encyclopedia of 7,700 Illustrations*, Paul Lee Tan (Garland, TX: Bible Communications Inc., 1979), p. 1387.

26. *A Diary of Readings*, John Baillie (NY: Collier Books, Macmillan Publishing Co., 1955), Day 202.

27. *Creative Living*, Autumn 1995, p. 20-24.

28. *The HarperCollins Book of Prayers*, Robert Van de Weyer, ed. (NY: HarperSanFrancisco, division of HarperCollins, 1993) p. 175-76.

29. *Amazing Grace*, Kenneth w. Osbeck (Grand Rapids, MI: Kregel Publications, 1993), p. 49.

30. *Give Your Life a Lift*, Herman W Gockel (St. Louis: Concordia Publishing House, 1968), p. 38-39.

31. *Amazing Grace*, Kenneth W Osbeck (Grand Rapids, MI: Kregel Publications, 1993), p. 228.

32. *The Treasure Chest*, Brian Culhane, ed. (San Francisco: HarperCollins, 1995), p. 10.

33. *Ibid*, p. 56.

34. *Prevention*, March 1996, p. 25- 26.

35. *The Treasure Chest*, Brian Culhane, ed. (San Francisco: HarperCollins, 1995), p. 88.

36. *Creative Living*, Summer 1993, p. 26.

37. *Newsweek*, January 22, 1996, p. 14.

38. *The Treasury of Inspirational Quotations & Illustrations*, E. Paul Hovey, ed. (Grand Rapids, MI: Baker Books, 1994), p. 168.

39. *The Treasure Chest*, Brian Culhane, ed. (San Francisco: HarperCollins, 1995), p. 92.

40. *Jewish Wisdom*, Rabbi Joseph Telushkin (NY: William Morrow and Company, Inc., 1994), p. 182-184.

41. *The World's Best Religious Quotations*, James Gilchrist Lawson, ed. (NY: Fleming H. Revell Company, 1930), p. 99.

42. *The Treasure Chest*, Brian Culhane, ed. (San Francisco: HarperCollins, 1995), p. 94.

43. *A Diary of Readings*, John Baillie (Collier Books, Macmillan Publishing Co., NY, 1955), Day 182.

44. *The Treasure Chest*, Brian Culhane, ed. (San Francisco: HarperCollins, 1995), p. 109.

45. *God Works the Night Shift*, Ron Mehl (Sisters, OR: Multnomah Books, 1994), p. 132- 133.

46. *The Treasure Chest*, Brian Culhane, ed. (San Francisco: HarperCollins, 1995), p. 146.

47. *Ibid*, p. 162.

48. *Webster's New World Dictionary of the American Language* (World Publishing Co., NY, 1968), p. 1258.

49. *The Upper Room* May-June 1996, p. 15.

50. *The New Yorker*, Nov. 20, 1995, p. 56-57, 59, 62-64.

51. *Scientific American*, July 1995, pp. 60-64.

52. *Knights Treasury of 2,000 Illustrations*, Walter B. Knight, ed. (Grand Rapids, MI: Eerdman Publishing, 1963), p. 274.

53. *American Health*, April 1996, pp. 76-78.

54. *Diamonds in the Dust* Joni Eareckson Tada (Grand Rapids, MI: Zondervan Publishing House, 1993), April 28 entry.

55. *Silent Strength*, Lloyd John Ogilvie (Eugene, OR: Harvest House, 1990), p. 129.

56. *Illustrations Unlimited*, James S. Hewett, ed. (Wheaton: Tyndale House, 1988) p. 25.

Additional copies of this book and other titles in the *Quiet Moments with God* series are available from your local bookstore.

In the Kitchen with God
Coffee Break with God
Breakfast with God
In the Garden with God
Daybreak with God
Tea Time with God
Through the Night with God
Christmas With God